CONSCIENCE AND THE CONSTITUTION

WITH

REMARKS ON THE RECENT SPEECH

OF THE

HON. DANIEL WEBSTER

IN THE SENATE OF THE UNITED STATES

ON THE SUBJECT OF

SLAVERY.

BY M. STUART

LATELY PROFESSOR IN THE THEOLOGICAL SEMINARY AT ANDOVER.

Δοῦλος ἐκλήθης, μή σοι μελέτω.—PAUL.

NEGRO UNIVERSITIES PRESS
NEW YORK

Originally published in 1850
by Crocker & Brewster

Reprinted from a copy in the collections
of the Brooklyn Public Library

Reprinted 1969 by
Negro Universities Press
A DIVISION OF GREENWOOD PRESS, INC.
NEW YORK

SBN 8371-2730-0

CONSCIENCE AND THE CONSTITUTION.

§ 1. *Introduction.*

I HAVE not selected a passage of Paul's first epistle to the Corinthians, to stand on my title page, without some hesitation. It is not because I am anxious about myself in the matter, that I have hesitated ; for let my motto be whatever it might, unless it were some favorite passage of the so-called anti-slavery party, it would probably be read by one portion of the community, in their present state of excitement, with strong forebodings of a pro-slavery effort. Let it be so, then, if it needs must be. I am willing, for myself, to shoulder the burden, and to stand under it if I can. But I rather shrink from putting the great apostle in the fore-front of such a battle, and exposing him to the contumely which any one else must meet with, who perils a declaration of the same purport as his, on his own responsibility. The reader who does not understand Greek, may find a translation of Paul's words, in the first clause of 1 Cor. 7: 21. There it stands, as translated, in the following words : ART THOU CALLED, BEING A SERVANT, CARE NOT FOR IT. Had I adopted some motto devised by myself, expressed it in other words of just the same import as those of the apostle, and then placed this instead of the words of Paul at the head of my little pamphlet, I should unquestionably find that a cataract of obloquy and indignation would speedily be pouring upon me. Still I could have dared to commit such a deed, had I not deemed it more to my purpose to quote what Paul says, than to quote myself.

That the great apostle himself may be brought into some disrepute, among a certain class of readers, by my exposure of his sen-

timents on the present occasion, is what I fear; and this is the only ground of the hesitation to which I have adverted. If I know my own heart, I would sooner expose myself to contumely, than occasion its coming upon him. Still, he has a better shield to protect himself than I have; and his words are likely to stand, unchanged and unrepealed, when the lips and the pens of revilers will be beyond the reach of harming him or his doctrine.

It is not my present object to go minutely here into the interpretation of the words I have quoted, and of the surrounding context. This belongs to another part of my little work. I have produced the words of Paul at the beginning of my inquiries and remarks, that such of my readers as still preserve a regard for the apostle's words and sentiments, may reflect on the advice which he gives to those who are under the yoke of slavery and who have to bear its pressure, and ask themselves, whether those who do *not* bear the yoke, and are in no danger of having it put upon them, may not seriously inquire, whether the μή σοι μηλέτω (*care not for it*) is not, on every ground, more applicable to them than to the sufferers. I know that there are many who will sneer at any one's suggesting, that a little more of the *laissez faire* would become them as believers in the Christian Scriptures. Yet such a suggestion seems to be needed; for even *religious* newspapers, not a few, appear utterly to ignore the apostle's words, and exhibit not a trace of ever having had cognition of them. Instead of "*not caring*," they occupy whole columns, yea whole broadsides, and now and then an *Extra* besides, with the most impassioned appeals and addresses, and with never ceasing contumely and vituperation, poured out in floods on all who, in this so-called *Land of Liberty*, use the liberty to differ from them in opinion. On all such, the rebuke of the apostle seems to be somewhat cutting. I cannot help it. I should be glad if that rebuke could be spared; for I do not court, and do not love, the business of applying it. I come to it with about as much reluctance, as Jeremiah (20: 7—10) felt to bring the message with which he was charged to the Jews. Probably I shall share the same fate that befel him.

Be this as it may, I have counted the cost, and am not satisfied that it should deter me from doing what I deem to be a sacred duty. It lies within my proper sphere of duty to hold up before the world the declarations and doctrines of God's eternal word; for I have

been a preacher of the gospel, according to the best of my knowledge and ability, for more than forty-five years. More than forty of these have been spent on the study of the Bible; and the consequence has been, that this book has taken a paramount place in my reverence, and in my sense of duty to obey it. Statesmen and jurists may discuss the great questions, now occupying all heads and all hearts, with much force and eloquence. They have done so, on both sides. Never, since the Declaration of Independence, and the formation of the United States Constitution, has there been so much deep feeling excited, or so much effort called forth. But there is, for all who profess a reverence for the Scriptures, another aspect of the great questions in agitation than that which statesmen and jurists, hampered by parliamentary tactics, can venture themselves to discuss. The majority in all our legislative bodies, as I fear, would look upon a man who should address *scriptural* arguments to them in the halls of legislation, as if he had risen from the dead, after having once been a member of the Long Parliament, in the time of Oliver Cromwell; and all the names which Butler has conjured up in his Hudibras, or Dr. South in his Sermons, or Tory writers in their diatribes, and have bestowed on the Puritan legislators, would be added to the name of the luckless wight who should once make such an appeal. Yet, forsooth, we are in a *Christian land!* Is this really so? Then may those whose life has been devoted to the teaching and diffusing of Christianity be pardoned, for sounding the words of prophets and apostles in the ears of our great community. I claim that right. I expect, however, to be condemned by some, and perhaps maligned by others, for exercising that right. No matter. It is but of little consequence what becomes of me, if the teachings of " the glorious Gospel of the blessed God" may come in their simplicity and power and authority before the public, in any manner that will attract their attention. It is too late for me to cast off the authority of that Gospel, or to shun my responsibility for proclaiming it. It would be reproachful to me in the highest degree, if I should desert the cause which I have so long and so deliberately espoused, in the day of assault or of peril.

By this time some of my readers will begin to inquire, perhaps with a degree of wonder, what has led me to such an introduction to what I have to say, on the present occasion. I feel that some apology for, or rather that some account of, my proem is due to

them.   I will narrate briefiy and simply what has called me out, and led me to the utterance of the preceding sentiments.

I have never been a *politician*, at least, I have never been what the world usually styles a politician.   In my early days, while in my college-studies, and afterwards in the study of the law, I was warmly engaged against the Jeffersonian politics and administration.   When I became a pastor of the First Church at New Haven, in Connecti-cut, I renounced all active pursuit of politics.   I never preached a political sermon in my life.   Usually I did not go to any meetings for the election of state or town officers.   My people were some-what divided in politics, and I did not like unnecessarily to offend those who differed from me, by voting against their wishes; for such was the violence of party in Jefferson-times, that offence would of course have been taken.   But I never shunned voting, because I feared the consequences as to myself.   It was principally because my vote was altogether unnecessary, and therefore (in my circum-stances) inexpedient, there being then an overwhelming majority in Connecticut of anti-Jeffersonians.   I have been more than forty years a resident and freeman in this commonwealth.   During all that period, I have never voted at the elections, more than some ten or twelve times.   In seasons of what I thought to be peril, I began to vote somewhat regularly; and it was under the imperial reign of Gen. Jackson, that I commenced such an exercise of my franchise-rights.   But I never preached politics, or taught them, in public. I have frequented the Lecture-room, in the Theological Seminary here, near forty years; yet I believe none of all my pupils will charge me with occupying their time in political lectures.   I have never written a political piece for our newspapers or magazines; except in one case now to be mentioned.   In that one case, I put my hand to a *critique* on a speech of Mr. Webster, delivered at Andover; and subjoined a defence of Mr. Webster's course, in the matter of continuing to hold office under President Tyler.   The people of the glorious old Bay State had been led, at that time, by the newspapers, (some of which were filled with inuendos against Mr. Webster made by interested politicians), into a disapprobation of Mr. Webster's course then, in like manner as I believe them now to be misled.   When the whole case was fairly laid before them, they hastened, as a body, and with that noble spirit which they cherish, to do him justice; I hope they will not refuse the like

justice on the present occasion, if as good an account can be given of Mr. Webster's course.

If it was a sin in me, who happened, (from circumstances unsought for and unexpected, and, I may add, quite peculiar in my life), to become acquainted with the true history of Mr. Webster's Secretaryship — if it was a sin to develop the matter to the public, so be it. I do not reproach myself as yet, however, for such a sin, because I have never been able to see any atrocity in helping to do justice to a man, to whom the public were so much indebted. After a short period, from that day to this, I have neither heard nor seen any reproach to Mr. Webster, from any respectable quarter, for the course he then pursued. Yet for myself I did not, for a time, escape severe censure, on the part of some of my fellow citizens. Anonymous letters full of reproaches were sent to me ; various newspaper paragraphs, for my edification, were carefully despatched to me by mail, fraught with bitter and sometimes malignant vituperation. Yet I survived. When the tornado had passed, I rose gently up, and finding no very serious bruises, I went quietly along my humble and peaceful way, as usual.

Since then, I have never meddled with politics. I have been engaged, when able to study, in other matters that I relished far more; and if I did not understand them better, it was my own fault. My increasing age and my many infirmities have given me a disrelish for the *mêlée* of political contest. It was not until within a few weeks, that I ever thought of approaching the arena of that contest, even near enough to look on and see what was doing. Unluckily for my quiet, the paper expressing approbation of Mr. Webster's late Speech was presented to me by a friend, and I was asked whether I agreed sufficiently with his views to sign it. My ready reply was in the affirmative. I put my name to the paper, and there I hope and wish it may stand. It is not a pledge, as I view the matter, that I am ready to support every shade of sentiment, on every topic upon which Mr. Webster's speech touches. That gentleman is the last man who would demand the surrender of their own individual views from his friends. But it is a pledge that I did, and it still signifies that I do, from the bottom of my heart, assent to, and agree with, all the important parts of Mr. Webster's reasoning in general ; and specially, it indicates my assent to his aim and desire to cherish our Union as inviolable, and to persuade both parties to make all

such mutual concessions as they can make, consistently with their consciences, for the sake of peace, of mutual good, and of firm consolidation. If I have erred in this case, it is at least in company with those who are not often impeached for want either of intelligence or integrity. Moreover, if "a man may be known by the company he keeps," then I am, for the present, in circumstances quite agreeable with respect to this matter. I will not say with Cicero, that 'I had rather err with philosophers, than think rightly with the populace;' but I must confess, that if error is imputable to me as to the present affair, my case is attended at least with not a few comforting alleviations. I can say to each of my fellow-signers, so far as I have the pleasure to know them, that, as to the matter now in question, *tecum amem vivere, tecum obeam libens.*

And now, what is the consequence of my alleged political *faux pas*? The public have little interest, indeed, to be informed of my individual experience; and were it not that they stand connected with my undertaking to write the following pages, I should of course pass them by in silence. But as the matter now is, what has befallen me may serve to cast some light, on the manner in which many of Mr. Webster's accusers manage their cause. Some other things, also, may perhaps have light cast upon them by what has befallen me. But I reserve, for the sequel, any remarks that I may find occasion to make respecting those matters.

Within a week after my name was set to the paper approving of Mr. Webster's Speech, I began to receive anonymous letters; and soon after, various newspapers of diverse character and complexion began to pour in. One anonymous letter states, that the writer once had much respect for my opinions and views, but that I have now showed him that he was much mistaken in me. Another says, that the only apology he can make for me is, that I have had a two years' sickness, which has doubtless very much impaired my mind; so that he can, on the whole, pity me rather than blame me. A third says, that I have now arrived at three score and ten, and like most men of that age, have become a child the second time; otherwise I never could have become the advocate of slavery. Another challenges me to show one text in all the Bible, which allows of slavery, or justifies my course in according with, and approving of, Mr. Webster's Speech. Another of my obliging friends, (it may be that he resides in our metropolis), sends me a slip of a newspaper,

on which is a paragraph, giving an account of the drove of slaves lately marched from Washington on Sunday, by Bruin, (I think this was the name), who charged some $1800 for a good looking young wench, whom he (Bruin) wished to sell to some gentleman ; and to this slip of information is added, in a note written in what I take to be a dissembled hand, the following monition : " You, by putting your name to Mr. Webster's paper, have put your seal of approbation on all this transaction; and you have moreover approved of the violation of the Sabbath, by the said Bruin." Another letter writer says, that 'I am neither more nor less than a downright wolf, in sheep's clothing.' Another wonders how a man could study the Bible for 40 years, and yet never have learned that slavery is a sin. These are only some of the many specimens.

As *unique* in its kind, I advert to one anti-slavery paper, (which it is needless to name, for there can be but one such), that was sent to me, as I suppose, by its philanthropic editor. In this, after a flood of Billingsgate on Mr. Webster's " SATANIC SPEECH," he includes within a square enclosed by funereal dressings, my name, that of Dr. Woods, of Dr. Emerson, and of President Sparks, and Professor Felton. Here we are — dead and gone — and (what is a little remarkable) all buried together. It is all well, and for one I am quite content; for a man, as people say, may be known by the company in which he is buried, as well as by those with whom he associates while living. But this is not all. In another paragraph, myself and my two venerable Colleagues are named together, and then the editor says : " These individuals have formerly been called preachers of evangelical truth ; but," he adds, " they are never more to be so named. They are to be classed with the Jewish high-priests, who accused the Saviour of the world at the bar of Pilate." — This, by the way, is merely a specimen; but thus much may suffice. I should not have noticed even this, but for a purpose that will appear in the sequel. I have, and can have, no contest with the editor of that paper. I wish to settle all the accounts, if any lie open, between me and him, by the simple remark, that he has my full and free consent to utter against me all the slander and contumely and vituperation that the compass of the English language will afford him the means of uttering — he is entirely welcome to ' let his tongue walk through the earth ' in its pestiferous howlings ; — and then, if he looks for any signs of excitement or impatience in me, he will find me as quiet

and peaceable and harmless as he could wish. He is in no danger of any suit for slander, nor even for blasphemy, (which, as most persons think, he not unfrequently utters), from me, or from my respected friends whom he has entombed with me. All I ask of him is, that he may never, on any occasion or by any means, be persuaded to utter one word in my praise, or in commendation of me. Should I see such a paragraph in his paper, I should begin forthwith to think, that his obituary notice had something ominous in it. At all events, I should severely tax my memory and my conscience to search diligently after, and find out if possible, what egregious folly or downright *betise* I had been committing, which had drawn down upon me the misfortune of his eulogium.

But there is a class of men different from all, who have thus far been brought to view, some of whom conduct papers highly respectable and useful in regard to most of their contents. Some of these, edited by even personal friends whom I heartily love and respect, have thought proper to make me and my colleagues the butt of allusion or remark, in nearly every number of their paper that has been issued since our unlucky deed of subscription. The pieces of this nature, if I ken aright, do not come from editorial hands, but from some of their zealous friends, who seem to consider themselves as officers in the corps of life-guards who keep watch in the temple of Liberty. After speaking of Mr. Webster as our *misrepresentative*, and as having done sacrifice to base electioneering purposes, and thrown out a gilded bait to catch the South ; after alleging that all the confidence of the Bay State in him is about defunct ; some confidential Ariel of the editors, who hails from Boston, and seems to know everything about everybody, goes on to say, ' that as to the merchants' (whose names are on Mr. Webster's testimonial), 'they cannot afford to have a conscience ; as to the politicians, their conscience varies with the wind ; and as to Professors, etc., their railroad must no longer run over the heights of Zion, [quære — Andover Hill?] but through the valley of Hinnom.' I do not, with the little that I know of exegesis, feel able to make out an interpretation of this last clause, and must therefore give it over to the reader to manage for himself as he best can. But there is another declaration of this sharp-sighted sentinel of the life-guard of Liberty, that I think I can cognize. He implicates all of us, who have subscribed the testimonial, in the accusation of being either the advocates of slavery, or

apologists for it. He says we make no more scruple "in riding over the ten commandments," than a merchant (he seems to have a peculiarly degrading opinion of merchants) does in riding to his cotton mills over the bales of southern cotton. In this, however, I think there is somewhat of a *faux pas.* At least, there seems to be disclosed a keenness of vision in seeing a mote in a neighbor's eye, without even dreaming that a beam may be in his own. When he says, or at least implies, that I, (I speak now only for myself, for others whom he has joined with me need no defence from me) — that I am the advocate or apologist of slavery, he speaks WHAT IS NOT TRUE; and thus he rides over one of the ten commandments which says: "Thou shalt not bear false witness against thy neighbor." When he appeals to the ten commandments as plainly and palpably decisive against all slavery, "he rides over" (to use his own choice and delicate expression) a certain *fourth* commandment, without once seeming to recollect, that this commandment requires men "to keep the Sabbath holy," and that "neither they, nor their sons, nor daughters, nor THEIR MEN-SERVANTS, nor THEIR MAID-SERVANTS, shall do any work" on that sacred day. In the ten commandments, then, *servants male and female* are recognized as a standing and permanent part or portion of the Jewish people. The fourth commandment prescribes their duties specifically *as servants.* And what is the conclusion from this? There is indeed no command here to *make* slaves; but it is equally true, that there is none to *unmake* them. One thing, however, is palpable, viz., that there is a cognizance of them in such a way as to render it quite certain, that Moses expected the Jewish nation to continue to have such a class of people as servants or slaves among them. He elsewhere gives them express liberty to do this, Lev. 25: 44—46. Who then *rides over* (cum pace aurium delicatiorum!) the largest number of commandments? Is it Ariel himself, or his vituperated neighbors? I take it for granted that the other nine commandments have *nothing about slavery in them ;* how is it, then, with the fourth? Or is there some *eleventh* commandment which we have rode over, because, being less sharp-sighted than Ariel, we did not see it?

Withal, this same life-guard watchman has a singular faculty of quoting and interpreting the Scriptures for his purpose; specially in applying them to the confounding of Mr. Webster and his friends. We shall have occasion by and by, to look a little into this part of

his development; not because of any special importance that attaches to what Ariel says or does, but because he has seized on thé same weapons of assault which are common to most who agree with him in anti-slavery notions, and which they brandish to the right and left with the expectation of either scattering all opposing forces by striking them with terror, or else of laying them low. We shall see, in due time, whether the weapons are sharp enough to do much execution, or well tempered enough to bear an opposing blow without shivering to pieces.

There are some other declarations from other assailants of Mr. Webster and his friends, in the same journal, which I intend to notice when a fitting opportunity occurs; not because I design to attack the journal, but because those declarations give expression to sentiments of late often avowed and widely proclaimed. I have referred to the journal in question, for the very reason that I regard it as edited for the most part in an able manner, and until quite recently as holding out fair promise of great and extensive usefulness.

It would not be worth my time or labor, to hunt up and bring forward the violent diatribes, which have issued of late from the second, third, and fourth rate papers; for their name is *legion.* I have referred to a paper highly respectable, in order to show, that matters are becoming somewhat serious, and that it is high time they should be examined on all sides. Statesmen and jurists will doubtless take care for themselves and their cause, as to what comes within their appropriate sphere. But in a *Christian* land, there are many — many thousands, sincerely desirous to know what light can be obtained from the Bible, to aid them in discerning and performing their duty, in times like these. To all such I have something to say; not so much in the way of apology for my own sentiments and course of conduct, as for the sake of " stirring up their pure minds by way of remembrance."

And now, after producing only a tithe of what has been brought before me, either to chastise or to edify me, may I be permitted to ask, why I should be doomed to such a lot? I can easily see, why Mr. Webster's Speech should have roused up the ire of those who call for emancipation to-morrow, and who are bent upon all possible measures to foreclose our unappropriated domains against the prospect of slavery, even at the risk of violating our plighted national

faith, of setting aside the solemn compacts which we have made, and of dissolving the Union and covering the land with blood. Such a speech, addressed to the sober, candid, law-loving, peace-loving, covenant-keeping freemen of our country, threatens much, no doubt, to the cause of the violent. Such Paixhan guns as he brings into the contest, threaten demolition to the tottering walls and brick-built citadels. No wonder they look with concern upon the issue of the contest ; and of course, no wonder that he should become the object with some of impassioned, and with others of embittered, attack. All this is easily explained. But why, in my peaceful retirement from the world, in my inaction and quietude as to politics, and while I am standing on the verge of the grave with one foot already in it — why I should have become, all at once, such a target to be fired at, seems to me somewhat inexplicable. Whom have I harmed ? And who can expect any harm from me, in such a condition ? However, straws (they say) show which way the wind blows. So an experience like mine shows the violence of party spirit that is abroad. In such of our journals as are published for the *canaille*, and well adapted moreover to gratify their taste, all this perhaps might be expected. But to find such violence in many of our *religious* papers, even in some which are among those of the first rank, this is an indication of a day approaching, which may be like that seen in vision by the Hebrew prophet, " a day of darkness and gloominess, a day of clouds and thick darkness, a day of trouble and distress, a day of wasting and of desolation." If my feeble hand can be employed in even giving a signal for halting a little time, until we can survey the ground more effectually before we hasten on in our forced march, yea, even for deliberating whether the present direction of our march had not better be abandoned, at least for a while — then my poor remnant of life will not have been spared in vain.

Such then, as I have shown above, is the state of things in which I undertake to speak a word of caution, well meant, although it may not perhaps be well spoken. If I look merely at the commotion which seems to surround me, I almost believe that I might be pardoned, if I should feel somewhat as the trident-god did, when he was called away from his quiet resting place in the depths of his watery domain, by the heavings of the ocean and the booming and dashing of its waves above, which had been lashed into fury and elevated to the skies, by the tornados that Eolus had let loose, with-

out the knowledge or consent of his Neptunian majesty. When the monarch raised his head above the surface of the deep, and saw its commotion, and the Trojan fleet like things of cork upon it, his first feeling was indignation; his second and better thought was, that he must, without delay, calm the raging element.

Quos ego — sed praestat componere fluctus.

If my first feeling was like his, it was very soon succeeded by the better second thought. I have no power indeed, such as Virgil attributes to Neptune, to calm the raging billows; but if I can pour even a little oil upon them, it may possibly be reckoned as a contribution of my mite, toward smoothing down their angry crests.

Let me, once for all, before I advance to the main objects that I have in view, here make a frank statement of my feelings in regard to a large class of men, who entertain views different from, and in some respects opposed to my own. Those who belong to this class, are not all of the like character; and therefore they should not in any way, either directly or by implication, be amalgamated together. I have already excepted one excellent journal and its editors, and stated my reason for making any reference or appeal to it. That its editors are high-minded Christian men, I cannot doubt. As little can I doubt that great numbers of the so-called Free Soil party are men of intelligence, of patriotism, and of integrity. They appear to me, to be adorned with every civil and social virtue. All this I most cheerfully concede and believe. Many of them, also, are men of exemplary Christian lives. Some of them, moreover, as we know from the developments which they have made, are men, whose eloquence can charm not only the mass of our citizens, but hold in breathless suspense our Senates and our Houses of Representatives. Not to go beyond the boundaries of our own Massachusetts, I have the pleasure of some personal acquaintance with a number of Free Soilers, who adorn private life by their virtues, and public life by their learning, their talents, and their eloquence. Nay, I could, if it were decorous, readily point to this man and that among them, and say with all my heart: *I nostrum decus!* Of such men I can fully believe, that their aim is good; that their principles (as to main positions) are humane, patriotic, becoming high-souled freemen. I believe those principles, bating some excesses to which excited feeling has carried them, are such as meet the approbation of a

tribunal higher than an earthly one can be. But in matters of exciting moment, where great and humane objects are sincerely believed to be at stake, it often happens, even to spirits of the nobler order, to become excited beyond the bounds of moderation and sober wisdom. I do not call this *crime*, in such men. I might almost say, that it is the fault, or rather the infirmity, of excessive virtue. But still, if the means which they employ to carry their cause through with success, are lacking in prudence, in sober foresight, in moderation, in justice, and in comity to opponents—then the public suffer far more from these distinguished and excellent men, than they would from all the efforts of the *Ledru Rollins* and the *Red Caps* who are in the midst of us. On the yeomanry of Massachusetts, at all events, Parisian Socialism and Parisian Liberty and Equality, are not likely to make much permanent impression. If the people of this State are in the end misled, it must be by men whose lives and talents have given them a commanding influence. Hence it is that I have ventured on the declaration, that when such men fall into excess of zeal, and lead the way to measures correspondent with this and indicative of it, the community suffer far more than they would be liable to suffer, from the excesses of all those who live on excitement, and are never gratified so much, as when they can allure or drive others into the like condition.

I have thus done, as I trust, the justice due to a large class of men among us. If at any time, in the hurry or excitement of writing, I should let drop one word that would seem to disagree with what I have now expressed, let such of my fellow-citizens as may be implicated in my remarks, draw their pen over that word, and be assured that it comes from inadvertence and not from design.

I wish I could speak in a similar tone of another class among us, who seem to be kindred spirits with the *Liberty-men* of Paris. I refer of course to such, and to the like of them, as have deluged me with the gall that I have briefly described in the pages above. What there is in all this, which is manly, patriotic, just, profitable, or decent, I am not able to see. By their fruits, at all events, they may be known, and by these they must expect to be judged. It would ill become me to occupy much time or paper with them. Such men, if I rightly judge, have little or nothing to lose, by a breaking up of the Union. No change can be much for the worse, so far as they are concerned; and the chance, as they believe, is,

that change may in some way present a better opportunity to help bring in *Socialism* upon us. When *property* (to use the language of their transatlantic coadjutor) becomes a *crime,* and equal division is made of the whole, then they may have "high life below stairs," as well as others can now have high life above stairs. If they will promise me now to keep their temper, I will tell them a short story, and then, wishing them better views and better feelings and more civility, I will bid them, for the present, a hearty adieu.

The story is this. In Jefferson-times, when party spirit was higher, if possible, than it now is, the inhabitants of New Haven, in Connecticut, where I then lived, were as a mass strong *Federalists.* As soon as Mr. Jefferson was fairly seated on his throne, and had got a Senate, a House of Representatives, and a Cabinet, obedient and entirely subservient to his will, he displaced a Collector of the Customs at New Haven, appointed by Washington, (a man of great integrity and distinguished ability for business, and then enjoying the highest confidence of his fellow citizens), and appointed in his room a gentleman above eighty years of age, a man indeed of unblemished character, but unfortunately the father of a real Jacobinic son. This son had been at Paris during the reign of terror, and, like Thomas Paine, with whom he sympathized both in religion and in politics, did all he could to aid the Mountain party. It was believed, of course, that he was the real *appointee;* and this was soon confirmed by his open appointment at his father's death. No man could have been more obnoxious to New Haven, at that period, than the son in question. The commotion of course was very great. Soon after the appointment in question came the Fourth of July. It was celebrated with a mixture of enthusiasm and of indignation. At the dinner which followed the exercises of the day, where some hundreds were seated at the table, an aged merchant of the town, a shrewd man and a high Federalist, was called on for a volunteer toast. He rose instantly and gave one thus: " Our New Collector, A. B. ! *When the political pot boils, the scum is sure to come to the top.*"

' Sed — paullo majora canamus.' I come now merely to mention further, that from some respected and cherished friends, I have received letters, stating their doubts and perplexities on the present agitated questions, and requesting me to point out, if I could, some way of *Christian* politics, in which they might conscientiously pro-

ceed. The tone of respect and kindness which pervaded these letters, induced me to give some special attention to the subject of a *Christian* examination. My undertaking was further stimulated, by other letters of a similar tenor ; and these assured me, that the writers of them knew many serious and conscientious persons, who were in the same predicament with themselves, and would be greatly relieved if the path of *Christian* duty could be pointed out. After some examination of the matter as an affair concerned with Christianity, I became so far satisfied in my own mind, that I could not well doubt for myself. When we get into this state, after a serious effort in the way of examination, we are apt to feel that what convinces ourselves, may perhaps help to convince others. The subject gradually grew upon me, until I finally concluded that I would make the attempt to communicate my views, provided no serious obstacle should be found in the way, and if I should continue to be in such a state, that I could perform the labor necessary.

My next step was, to see that Mr. Webster should be consulted on the question, whether he would have any objections to my canvassing his speech. I did this through the medium of a friend ; for between Mr. Webster and myself no communications had yet passed. That friend gave him my letter, on his coming to Boston. The reason why I took pains to get Mr. Webster's views, was, on my part, a regard to delicacy and respect, and not for the sake of forming my own opinions, which had already been formed. The letter of mine, that was put into his hand, stated merely that my special design was, if he concurred, to take a *Christian* view of the agitated questions. In answer to my letter, Mr. Webster sent me the following communication, which, with his consent, I shall here subjoin, premising merely, that I should have omitted the first paragraph, had it not been a plain case, from the temper of the times, that any omission would be supposed by some readers, to have been filled up with matter which it would not do to publish, and which some might guess was very different from what Mr. Webster has actually written. If I be amenable at the bar of delicacy, for publishing a paragraph expressive of kindness and regard to myself, I hope to obtain a pardon, in case of condemnation, for the reason already stated. Here is the letter :

" Boston, April 31, 1850.

" My Dear Sir, — I cannot well say how much pleasure it gave me to see a name so much venerated and beloved by me as yours is, on the letter recently received by me from friends in Boston and its vicinity, approving the general object and character of my speech in the Senate, of the seventh of March. I know the conscientiousness with which you act on such occasions, and therefore value your favorable sentiments the more highly.

" Is it not time, my dear Sir, that the path of Christian duty, in relation to great and permanent questions of Government, and to the obligations which men are under to support the Constitution and the fundamental principles of the Government under which they live, should be clearly pointed out? I am afraid we are falling into loose habits of thinking upon such subjects ; and I could wish that your health and strength would allow you to communicate your own thoughts to the public.

" We have established over us, as it appears to me, a much better form of Government than may ordinarily be expected in the allotments of Providence to men ; and it appears to me that the consciences of all well meaning and enlightened individuals, should rather be called upon to uphold this form of Government, than to weaken and undermine it, by imputing to it objections, ill considered and ill founded, dangerous to the stability of all governments, and not unfrequently the offspring of over heated imaginations.

" Allow me to conclude, my dear Sir, by offering you my highest respects, and my affectionate good wishes for your health and happiness."   DANIEL WEBSTER.

Rev. Mr. Stuart.

I should, of course, have spared the public all this, so far as I myself am concerned. But I well knew, that concert between Mr. Webster and me would be charged upon my pamphlet, and it would be put mainly to his account. He has more than once, in some journals which have a Christian name and wear a Christian face, been taunted with getting up a subscription-paper, declarative of approbation by his particular friends, in order to keep himself in countenance, and to prop him up in his falling condition. Nay, I have repeatedly seen statements, that the whole State of Massachusetts had been scoured, from Cape Cod to Berkshire, in order to get underwriters for him ; that every store and shop and stall and bar-room and kennel had been rummaged, in order to increase the number of vouchers for his speech ; and that after all the running to and fro over the whole land by his partizans, they had been able to collect from the whole Bay State, only between seven and eight

hundred persons, who were willing to vouch for the propriety of his speech. Now those who can say this, of course can say anything. Those who have said it, at least some of them, know that no signers were sought for or wished, except from Boston and its suburbs. Andover, at all events, is at the greatest distance from Boston, where any application for subscription was made; and there but in a few cases. The names on the list are the pledge of all this. If there are any names, (I have not seen the full list, and therefore speak conditionally), on the subscription paper, which belong at any distance from Boston, it comes about merely from the persons' being in Boston when the paper was carried round. What could be the inducement to publish such a palpable falsehood, it would be diffi-cult, in one point of view, to say; but still, not very difficult in another. *Delenda est Carthago.* If Mr. Webster's reasoning cannot be answered, (and this is somewhat of a hard task), he must in some other way be put down. At all events, this last point must be car-ried; and what would help more in the present exigency, than to persuade the public, that Mr. Webster has lost the confidence of his own State? No matter, think they, if the falsehood is discovered and exposed, by and by. Justice has a lame foot, and moves very slowly; and she will not come with her scorpion lash, until we have realized all that we hoped for. It may be so, I answer; but when justice does come — what then? Can you, who have made such statements to the public, expect any longer to be trusted by them? The real truth seems to be, that we are acting over again the scenes of old Athens, in the days of Aristides. His rival, Themistocles, went about the whole city, whispering all manner of surmises against him, so that at length the populace were ready to thrust out the best and most distinguished man in their commonwealth. On the day when the votes of Athens were to decide the fate of Aristides, he asked one of the citizens on his way to the voting-hall, to whom he was personally unknown, how he was going to vote. He told him he should vote to banish Aristides. Why? said he, what has he done? Why nothing, replied the simple clown, that I know of; but I am tired of hearing every body call him the *Just.* So is it, I fear, among us at the present moment. The man who has commanded more listening ears, and made more hearts beat high, these twenty years past, than any other man in our great community, is called upon by the spirit of the Levellers to come down to their humbler

place, and take his lot with them. "*A bas le Sénateur!* There are other men who have as good a right to reign as you; and if we cannot bring you to a level by argument, we can do it by contumely and vituperation." This is the brief, but, I am pained to say that I feel constrained to believe, the true history of the matter.

Mr. Webster, forsooth, asking for underwriters in *politics*, and drumming up all Massachusetts to get them! Tell it not in Gath! It is neither true that he would ask for any such thing, nor true that his friends would condescend to devise and execute any such measure.

Let those who are doing such deeds of violence against fact and truth, call to mind, that Athens, when she had banished her Aristides for six years, felt obliged to recall him before the end of that period, and to give him her highest confidence and her posts of highest honor. Let them call to mind, that when the immortal Æschylus, in one of his lofty and glowing tragedies, introduced a sentence replete with eulogy of moral goodness and integrity, every eye, in the assemblage of those very Athenians who once voted for his banishment, was filled with tears of emotion, and was spontaneously fixed upon Aristides, who was then present. And so will it be with us, if the impetuous zeal of the present hour is to march forward until it gains its ultimate end. We are full surely preparing for a future repentance.

In one word, no man who regards truth has any right to say, that Mr. Webster has procured his friends to prop him up, in the way of subscription to a paper commending his speech, or that he has enlisted me now in his service. He has not lifted one finger, in the way of accomplishing either object. And yet, in the way of helping to depreciate him, a respectable journal asks: ' How is it that his political Orthodoxy needs vouchers? What is the matter with it? What if Dr. Woods should be vouched for on the score of *Orthodoxy*, by an Association of Ministers in Boston, or elsewhere? Would it not seem passing strange, that he was in need of such vouchers?' Yes it would, I answer, in present circumstances. But suppose Dr. Woods were unjustly assailed in different quarters, and many things were laid to his charge without any foundation or good reason; would it be strange if Dr. Woods's friends, who best know him, should rally, and volunteer their united testimony to put down the false accusations? No, it would be strange if they did not do so.

Why then may not Mr. Webster's friends who have long been his neighbors and best know him, in a time of unrestrained and unmeasured obloquy, rally around him, and bid him *God-speed* in his patriotic and noble course? They may do so; they have done so; and they are none the less resolved to hold on in their course, by any false statements, so long as what they consider to be palpable injustice is done to him.

But — enough of preface to my little book, unless the porch is to be larger than the building. I can only say, once more, that little if any of all this preface would have been written, had not the facts, now brought into view, contributed to throw light on the character of the times, and on the *moderation* and *comity* of some of those, whose opinions I expect to call in question. I must say, however, that I do not think the old proverb: "A man is known by the company he keeps," will apply, in the present case, to a large portion of those who dissent from Mr. Webster's views. It is an unblest, unnatural union — this union of these with those — one of the matches *not* made in heaven, that has brought together such reputable men as I have described above (p. 14), and such as many of those are, who have *loaded* me with such favors as I could well dispense with, (see p. 8 seq.), and for which I am not specially grateful. But such is the doom of party spirit, when it runs high. We may and should regret it; but I see no way to prevent it.

One more remark, and I shall proceed to my main business. This is, that I have learned to suspect, that there is some distrust in the strength and goodness of their cause, when men begin to vituperate, to slander, and to satirize those, who are opposed to their views. I have seen some service, in my day, in the wars of pens, and sometimes felt obliged to act as well as to see. Long ago I learned by observation, a lesson that impressed itself deeply on my mind. Those who feel a sober conviction from serious and repeated examination, that the views which they cherish are well grounded, and will bear assault without any lasting harm, are very apt to keep quiet, and cool, even when listening to declamation and obloquy. Why not? They are in no real danger. It is for those who are afraid that their underpinning may give way, and bring down the whole superstructure upon them, to keep constantly on the *qui vive*, and to make so much noise and bustle as will turn the attention of the public to the commotion, rather than to the foundations of the

edifice whence the noise proceeds. One part expect to be heard for much speaking; another, for loud speaking; another, for their ingenuity in the formation of vituperative epithets; and another, for their skill in substituting fiction for fact. Some write for a reason as good as Voltaire assigned, for a false statement (which however was quite *piquante*) in one of his histories. When advertised of the matter by an acquaintance of his, who was surprised to see it, he very coolly replied: 'My dear Sir, *I must be read.*' Some of these writers think in like way, and are well prepared to say: *Si non cœlum —Acheronta movebo.* But — all badinage apart — it is my sober conviction that very much less of excitement would now exist, did not the array of Mr. Webster's arguments appear so formidable. If he is willing to risk his reputation and honor, in uttering sentiments which every tyro in the *Free Soil* political ranks can refute, why then *lassez faire.* There is no need of attacking him. He is undoing himself as fast as his enemies could wish. But — do they feel so? Do they believe all this? Not a word of it. It is the Paixhan guns that they fear, when directed against chinky walls and citadels of mouldering brick.

My preface is through. I advance, then forthwith to the first part of my main design. This is,

§ 2. *To exhibit the attitude of Slavery as presented by the Old Testament.*

I must prepare the way for this exhibition, by a few remarks on the positions assumed by the *anti-slavery* party (so called) of the present day.

One leading position, a thousand thousand times repeated, is, that slavery, on the part of the master is a crime of the first magnitude; a real *malum in se;* a *crimen capitis;* a misdeed to be placed by the side of murder, adultery, robbery, treason, and the like. Often is this position advanced without making any distinction between the case of an involuntary master of slaves, (one who has inherited them and cannot, without the most imprudent risk of doing them injury, free them immediately in the circumstances in which they are), and those who have trafficked in them, or been concerned with the piratical business of bringing them away from Africa. The bare possession is, as they assert, an outrage; the bare relation is in itself a

sin. Immediate repentance and the proclamation of their freedom are duties to be done without the least delay. Stolen goods, the fruit of robbery, they say, are not to be retained a single hour, after the man who has obtained them has come to a proper sense of his duty.

Is all this really so? Is this alleged *malum in se*, a case so entirely clear as it is said to be, in all its extent and in all its ramifications? Will the Scriptures bear us out in this position? For after all, this must be the ultimate test to which all sincere Christians are bound to appeal. A thorough Protestant, at least, professes to believe, that " the Scriptures are the *sufficient* and only rule of faith and practice."

We begin our investigation with the Old Testament. Our first object is to develop the matter as it there stands; our next will be to subjoin some remarks on this development.

Of the great *antiquity* of slavery no one can doubt. The curse of Noah that lighted on the progeny of the unfilial Ham, was, that Canaan his son should be a *servant of servants* unto his brethren, Gen. 9: 25. This language, uttered soon after the flood, shows plainly that *slavery* had an existence before the flood ; for otherwise, it would not have been intelligible. No wonder it was so, " for the earth was filled with violence " (Gen. 6: 11) ; and slavery, for the most part, originates in violence, and has its deepest foundation in the simple but utterly unjust principle, that *might is right*.

Under many modifications, however, did slavery exist among the patriarchs of the Jewish nation. Abraham, " the father of the faithful," (when his nephew Lot was taken captive, his goods rifled, and himself carried off by marauding banditti), could bring into the field 318 armed and disciplined servants, born in his own great household, and make pursuit after the robbers, and disperse them, Gen. 14: 12—16. If one *fifth* be taken as the proportion among his servants of such men, viz. those who were capable of bearing and using arms, Abraham's family of slaves must have consisted of at least 1590 persons ; somewhat larger, I think, than any like family among our fellow citizens of the South. However, we must call to mind here, that Abraham's relation to these slaves was somewhat different from that of master to slave among us. The patriarch resembled, in his mode of life, the Nomades who still roam over the very country from which he sprung. The Sheikhs among them often have under

their control a whole tribe; and this tribe stand in such relation to their Sheikh, as the serfs under the old feudal law bore to their master. Bodily service in the way of labor when needed, and special military service in predatory and warlike expeditions, were always at the command of the master. So, moreover, did the administration of justice, and the power of life and death, pertain to him. But in the East, where servitude everywhere prevails, the slaves, for the most part, are generally treated with less rigor, and more as human beings should be treated, than they are in most countries called *Christian*. Especially do the *family-servants* find much favor in the eyes of their master. It is a frequent custom now, among the Persians for example, to bestow legacies on this class of slaves, and nearly always (if they have behaved well) to give them their freedom. See how exactly the case of Abraham illustrates this. He had no child until he was 100 years of age; and in making arrangements for the disposition of his property after his death, (before the promise of a son), he had made the steward of his house his heir who was a slave of Damascene origin, one born as a slave in his own house, Gen. 15: 2, 3. When, therefore, the example of the patriarch is referred to as justifying modern slavery, it should be remembered, that what the Arabian Sheikhs now are to their petty tribes, Abraham was to his 1590 servants.

One striking circumstance respecting slavery, quite revolting to our occidental and Christian views, deserves mention here. If the mistress of the house was childless, a favorite female slave was selected by her, and offered by her to her husband, to take the place of a wife. In case of offspring, the children of this slave were regarded as the children of the real wife. The case of Sarah and Hagar fully illustrates this, as told in Gen. 16: 1—3; and it was as Abraham's son, that the blessing came upon Ishmael, Gen. 17: 20. And when Abraham was about to die, he bestowed gifts on all his sons born of his concubines, and sent them away free from the domination of his heir, Gen. 25: 5, 6.

Of Isaac, the patriarch's regular heir, we read that he "had in possession a great store of servants," Gen. 26: 14. When Rachel, the favorite wife of Jacob, Isaac's son, found herself childless, she, like Sarah, gave to her husband her favorite female servant, in order that she might claim the rights of a mother, and this slave bore to Jacob two sons, Gen. 30: 1—8. Jacob's other wife Leah, although

she had already borne four sons, was so ambitious of outstripping her rival in progeny, that she too gave her handmaid to her husband; and she increased the motherly rights and joy of the mistress, by bearing two sons, Gen. 30: 9—13. Thus *four* of the twelve patriarchs were the sons of favorite bond-women, voluntarily substituted by lawful wives to take their own place. Nor do we ever find any difference made between those four and the other sons, as to the treatment they received, or the rank which they held.

Such was, and still is, the manner of slavery in the East. If an appeal be made to the example of the patriarchs in order to defend slavery, we must carry the matter through all their domestic arrangements. We should soon come in this way to the conclusion, that wives among us, not blest with children, may readily supply the deficiency, as Sarah, and Rachel, and Leah did, and the children thus born would become lawful heirs of the husband; a matter that now and then would be of serious importance to slighted wives, for whom no adequate provision had been made. But modern Christian views have introduced a very different taste and manner of conduct among our wives. Few, even if it were allowable, would be so fond of the mere name of mother, as to give up their husbands to their servants. If we appeal to the patriarchs to justify slavery, then why not appeal to them in order to justify polygamy and concubinage? Undoubtedly they neither thought nor intended to do wrong in either of the cases that are before us. But this will not justify us in imitating them. The gospel has given us better light.

I shall enter into no argument here in defence of the patriarchs, as to the usages now in question. In one sense they do not concern us; for the blessed God, by his gospel, having scattered the darkness of early ages, has made us to walk in the clear light of the Sun of Righteousness, so that polygamy and concubinage are no more regarded, in Christian lands, as lawful or proper. Perhaps we may see, before we are through, that slavery is as little commanded or even permitted by the highest form of Christianity, as those practices. Still, it is proper to say in relation to the patriarchs, that every man's conduct is to be judged of in most cases, at least in some good measure, by the light he has, and by the age and circumstances in which he lived. When Sir John Malcolm was introduced as English ambassador to the Shah of Persia, the first question after the formal salutations were over was· How many wives has the

Shah of England got? Sir John replied: May it please your Majesty, ONE. One, said the astonished monarch, One? Why not more? Because, replied the ambassador, our customs and laws permit but one. Then, rejoined the Shah with great emphasis, nothing would tempt me to be the Shah of England. Had George the Fourth then been on the throne of England, Sir John might have replied, that the Shah of England would very much like to be in his Persian Majesty's place; for the latter had then 1800 wives and 100 sons. Instead of this being regarded by him, however, as a disgrace and a stain upon his character, he gloried in his preëminence above all who had been seated on the throne of Persia, in respect to the multitude of his wives and children.

This now is a specimen of *oriental* feeling. Much of the like feeling is evident even in the patriarchal history that has just been brought to view. Christianity alone makes marriage a sacred, an exclusive, an inviolable compact. Christianity alone has brought us back to the primitive state of man, in regard to this matter. Adam had but one Eve. But Abraham and the other patriarchs lacked our light. If they had possessed it, there cannot be a doubt that they would have followed its guidance, and rejoiced in it. Noble traits of character they had; but it needs the blessed gospel of God to make men " perfect, thoroughly furnished unto every good work." What Christ has *commanded* is our rule; and not what the patriarchs *did*, who lived when the light was just beginning to dawn.

We proceed at once to the Mosaic Constitution and Laws. The foundation of all the ordinances respecting slavery, is disclosed in Ex. xxi. But it should be noted here, that the regulations there exhibited have respect only to *Hebrew* servants, and not to those of foreign origin. It will be seen by an inspection of this chapter, that Moses, at the outset, provided for many mitigations of the usual rigors of slavery. Hebrew *men* might be bought and sold; yet only for the term of *six* years. The seventh year set them free. If the man, who was sold into bondage, had a wife and children before the sale, they also were freed with him. If he married a wife given him by his master, then she and her children were to be regarded as belonging to the master; unless the year of jubilee intervened, when all were to be free, Lev. 25: 39—41. If a man purchased a concubine, and lost his fondness for her, then she might be redeemed by her friends for a moderate sum. If he betrothed her to his son,

then he must treat her after the manner of daughters.   If the master took another in her room, her support and comfort and conjugal rights were not to be disregarded.   If they were, then she was *ipso facto* free.   If a man should smite his servant, male or female, so that he or she should die, his punishment was made imperative.   If, however, the smitten servant survived, and continued for some time, the presumption was that the master did not mean to kill; and the loss of the slave was regarded as his fine.   If a man smote out an eye or a tooth, i. e. if he in any way maimed his man-servant or maid-servant, then freedom was of course to follow.   I subjoin the passages here, for convenience' sake, which show the ground of the preceding statements :

Ex. 21: 2. If thou buy a Hebrew servant, six years he shall serve: and in the seventh he shall go out free for nothing. (3) If he came in by himself, he shall go out by himself: if he were married, then his wife shall go out with him. (4) If his master have given him a wife, and she have borne him sons or daughters, the wife and her children shall be her master's, and he shall go out by himself. . . . . (7) And if a man sell his daughter to be a maid-servant, she shall not go out as the men-servants do. (8) If she please not her master, who hath betrothed her to himself, then shall he let her be redeemed; to sell her unto a strange nation he shall have no power, seeing he hath dealt deceitfully with her. (9) And if he have betrothed her unto his son, he shall deal with her after the manner of daughters. (10) If he take him another *wife*, her food, her raiment, and her duty of marriage shall he not diminish. (11) And if he do not these three unto her, then shall she go out free without money. . . . . (20) And if a man smite his servant, or his maid, with a rod, and he die under his hand; he shall be surely punished. (21) Notwithstanding, if he continue a day or two, he shall not be punished: for he *is* his money. . . . . (26) And if a man smite the eye of his servant, or the eye of his maid, that it perish; he shall let him go free for his eye's sake. (27) And if he smite out his man-servant's tooth, or his maid-servant's tooth; he shall let him go free for his tooth's sake.

Of the treatment of slaves, something will be said in the sequel. It is proper to show, first, HOW MEN MIGHT BECOME SLAVES. (*a*) As a general thing, all *captives in war* were regarded as slaves, I believe, by all the ancient world; see Num. 31: 18, 32, 35, 40. But this does not apply to the case now before us, which is that of *Hebrew* slaves, Deut. 20: 14. 21: 10—12. (*b*) *By debt;* see 2 K. 4: 1. Is. 50: 1. Matt. 18: 25. (*c*) *By theft;* for the thief, if poor, was sold to repay the property which he had stolen. (*d*) *By birth,* when the mother was a slave; so that *children of the house,* or *born*

in the house, became as it were a kind of proper name for slaves; see Gen. 14: 14. 15: 3. 17: 23. 21: 10. Ps. 86: 16. 116: 16. (*e*) *By sale and purchase*. A man might sell himself (Lev. 15: 47), which, however, was not very common; or another who owned a slave might sell him; but the seventh year, and above all the jubilee year, broke the bonds of slavery; Lev. 25: 25—28, 39—41. (*f*) There was one way more of making slaves, viz. by stealing and selling them. This the law of Moses punished with *death*, Ex. 21: 16. Deut. 24: 7. The latter passage, however, shows that this law, in its primary design, applied only to the stealing of *Hebrews:* "If a man be found stealing any of *his brethren of the children of Israel*, etc." Yet that this extended to the slaves of foreign origin resident among the Hebrews, I doubt not. All servants of every kind were to be circumcised, Gen. 17: 12—14; and thus they became quasi-members of the Jewish community, and rested, like the Jews, on the Sabbath and on feast days, i. e. they partook of their religious privileges, Ex. 20: 10. Deut. 5: 14. 12: 17, 18. 16: 10, 11. If one of these servants was stolen, then, it would seem at least probable that the law was to be extended to his purloiners. But to quote these passages, as is every day done, to show directly the criminality of *foreign* slave making, is doubtless uncritical and unfounded, as it respects the original and main object of the Jewish law. Yet the *spirit* of that law, (now the partition between Jew and Gentile is broken down), would seem to be fairly applicable to *all* cases of man-stealing. All men are now as much, or at any rate as really, our brethren, as the Hebrews in Moses' time were brethren of each other. Hence the law, almost if not quite universal among Christian nations, which makes foreign man-stealing piracy, is, in my view, altogether in the spirit, although not after the letter, of the Mosaic statutes.

We come next to THE TREATMENT OF SLAVES. (*a*) A Hebrew sold for poverty, i. e. for debt, was not to be treated with rigor as a bond-servant, but as a hired servant; and he and all his were to be free on the coming of jubilee-year, Lev. 25: 39—43. (*b*) The master who killed his (Hebrew) slave, was to be punished in an exemplary manner, Ex. 21: 20, 21. (*c*) A master who maimed his servant, was compelled to set him free, Ex. 21: 26, 27. (*d*) Slaves should enjoy the rest of the Sabbath, Ex. 20: 10. Deut. 5: 14; and be invited to the solemn feasts and festivals, Deut. 12: 17, 18. 16: 10, 11. (*e*) They should

have a comfortable support, Deut. 25: 4, as expounded by Paul 1 Tim. 5: 18. 1 Cor. 9: 9, 10. (*f*) As stated above, and apparent in the passages there quoted at length, every seventh year, and the jubilee-year, severed the bonds of slavery; see also in Lev. 25: 39—41. (*g*) It appears, by a comparison of Lev. 25: 49 and 2 Sam. 9: 10, that slaves were permitted the enjoyment of some little property as their own.

Such is the picture of the slavery of Hebrews among Hebrews. There remains, however, one extraordinary circumstance in the legislation of Moses, in relation to this subject. When Moses came out of Egypt and gave the law of Sinai, he declared that Hebrew *men-servants* should be free after six years; but not a word of this nature is said, as to the *female-servants*. But after 40 years, when on the borders of the promised land, he made the law, which before was applicable only to males, equally applicable thenceforth to *females*. Very plainly are the prudence and sagacity of the Jewish lawgiver developed here. Such was the universal feeling on the subject of slavery, when he began to legislate, that it would have been hazarding disobedience and rebellion, if Moses had freed *females* as well as males, after six years' service. Their universal degradation in the East, rendered such a measure revolting to the Jews, and quite impracticable. But when Moses had been moulding the manners and customs of the Hebrew nation for 40 years, he felt that this matter ought to be placed on its proper basis. Accordingly, Deut. 15: 12—15 declares, that a Hebrew *bond-man* or *bond-woman* shall go free on the coming in of the seventh year, and that they should be *liberally* supplied by their master, from the flocks, and the grain-floor, and the wine-press. A truly noble advance in legislation, and worthy of such a man!

Why now did not Moses do this thing at Sinai? He had both the power and the right; for he was divinely commissioned. Why then did he not do it? Simply, I answer, because he had common sense and judgment enough to see, that legislation could not change the established internal structure of a nation or commonwealth in a day. There must be a *preparation* for obedience, before the law would or (morally speaking) could be obeyed. How different such a policy was from that which is trumpeted by the immediate Emancipationists of our day, it needs no words of mine to show. However, the great Jewish legislator seems to be a very insignificant

person in the view of many of these zealous gentlemen. They think that his eyes were but half opened, if indeed they were open so far. Of course, they let this matter of his alone, as much as possible, and contrive to *ignore* it in all feasible ways. No wonder. It is a precedent of frowning aspect on all heated rashness and extravagance, specially in respect to great questions where national and universal usages of long standing and deep root are concerned.

One more passage in the Mosaic code claims our particular notice. This is in Deut. 23: 15, 16, and runs thus: "Thou shalt not deliver unto his master the servant which is escaped from his master unto thee. He shall dwell with thee, even among you, in that place which he shall choose in one of thy gates, where it liketh him best; thou shalt not oppress him."

The first inquiry of course is: Where does his master live? Among the Hebrews, or among foreigners? The language of the passage fully develops this, and answers the question. He " has escaped from his master unto the Hebrews (the text says—*thee*, i. e. Israel); *he shall dwell with thee, even among you . . . in one of thy gates."* Of course, then, he is an *immigrant,* and did *not* dwell *among them* before his flight. If he had been a Hebrew servant, belonging to a Hebrew, the whole face of the thing would be changed. Restoration, or restitution, if we may judge by the tenor of other property-laws among the Hebrews, would have surely been enjoined. But be that as it may, the language of the text puts it beyond a doubt that the servant is a *foreigner,* and has fled from a *heathen master.* This entirely changes the complexion of the case. The Hebrews were God's chosen people, and were the only nation on earth which worshipped the only living and true God. On this ground, as they were the living depositary of the oracles of God, great preference was given to them, and great caution exercised, to keep them from all tangling alliances and connections with the heathen. In case a slave escaped from them and came to the Hebrews, two things were to be taken into consideration, according to the views of the Jewish legislator. The first was, that the treatment of slaves among the heathen was far more severe and rigorous, than it could lawfully be under the Mosaic law. The heathen master possessed the power of life and death, of scourging, or imprisoning, or putting to excessive toil, even to any extent that he pleased. Not so among the Hebrews. *Humanity* pleaded, then, for the protection of the fugitive.

The second and most important consideration was, that only among the Hebrews could the fugitive slave come to the knowledge and worship of the only living and true God. The clause which says : " Thou shalt not oppress him," of course means, that he shall be denied none of the privileges of a resident in the land, and that he shall not be subjected to peculiar taxation or labor. The verses before us do not say, that such a refugee servant shall be circumcised ; but the admission of him to the privileges of a freeman implies this. The servants of Hebrews, whether of domestic or foreign origin, were all to be circumcised, Gen. 17: 12—15. Of course the admitted denizen, in the present case, would be required to comply with such an injunction. By the rite in question he became incorporated into the Jewish theocratical commonwealth, and therefore entitled, as even bond-men were, to all its religious privileges. Moses, therefore, would not suffer him to be forced back into the darkness of heathenism, nor allow that he should be delivered up to an enraged heathen master. Was he not in the right ?

But if we now put the other case, viz., that of escape from a *Hebrew* master, who claimed and enjoyed Hebrew rights, is not the case greatly changed ? Who could take from him the property which the Mosaic law gave him a right to hold ? Neither the bond-man himself, nor the neighbor of his master to whom the fugitive might come. Reclamation of him could be *lawfully* made, and therefore must be enforced.

With this view of the matter before us, how can we appeal to the passage in question, to justify, yea even to urge, the retention of fugitive bond-men in our own country? We are one nation — one so-called *Christian* nation. Christianity is a *national* religion among us. I do not mean, that all men are real Christians, or that Christianity is established by law; but I mean, that immeasurably the greatest part of our population, North and South, profess to respect Christianity, and appeal to its precepts as a test of morals, and as furnishing us with the rules of life. What State in the Union does not at least tacitly admit Christianity to hold such a place?

When a fugitive bond-man, then, comes to us of the North, from a master at the South, in what relation do we of the North stand to that Southern master? Are our fellow-citizens and brethren of the South, to be accounted as *heathen* in our sight ? No, this will never do. I know not what the proportion of real Christians in the

South may be, compared with those of the North; but this I do know from personal observation made at the South, to some extent, and from a considerable acquaintance with people of the South, that there are among them many warm hearts and active hands in the cause of true Christianity. There is no State where such persons may not be found, and many of them too. A bond-man, fleeing from them to us, is a case of just the same kind as would have been presented among the Hebrews, if a Hebrew bond-man had fled from the tribe of Judah to that of Benjamin. We do *not* send back the refugee from the South to a *heathen* nation or tribe. There is many a *Christian* master there, and many too who deal with their servants as immortal beings. It may be, that the fugitive has left a severe and cruel master, who will wreak his vengeance upon him for escaping. And it may be, also, that if the fugitive takes up his abode *here*, he will find those who will maltreat him, and defraud him, and do other grievous things. Crimes of this sort have not as yet quite vanished from the North. But be the master as he may, since we of the North are only other tribes of the same great commonwealth, we cannot sit in judgment on cruel masters belonging to tribes different from our own, and having, by solemn compact, a separate and independent jurisdiction in respect to all matters of justice between man and man, with which no stranger can on any pretence whatever intermeddle. We pity the restored fugitive, and have reason enough to pity him, when he is sent back to be delivered into the hands of enraged cruelty. But if he goes back to a lenient and a Christian master, the matter is less grievous. The responsibility, however, for bad treatment of the slave, rests not in the least degree on us of the North. The Mosaic law does not authorize us to reject the claims of our fellow countrymen and citizens, for strayed or stolen property — property authorized and guarantied as such by Southern States to their respective citizens. These States are not *heathen*. We have acknowledged them as *brethren* and *fellow citizens* of the great community. A fugitive from them is not a fugitive from an idolatrous and polytheistic people. And even if the Bible had neither said nor implied anything in relation to this whole matter, the solemn *compact* which we have made, before heaven and earth, to deliver up fugitives when they are *men held to service* in the State from which they have fled, is enough to settle the question of *legal* right on the part of the master, whatever we

may think of his claim when viewed in the light of Christianity. But of this, more in the sequel.

In the meantime, I cannot quit this topic, without adding a few remarks on the assumption, that every slave-holder must be denied the title of a Christian, and denied the regard which is due to a Christian brother. It is not too much to say, that no man, in his sober senses, can believe or say, that there are no Christians in the South, who are owners of slaves. There are thousands of masters and mistresses, of exemplary Christian lives and conversation. There are many thousands, moreover, who have never been taught to doubt, and never have doubted, the lawfulness of slavery. They have felt that they violated no sacred obligation in holding slaves, provided they should treat them in a Christian manner. Whether they have neglected their duty in putting by all discussion of the subject, and all serious examination into it, is another and a different question. I suppose there are Christians elsewhere, besides in the South, who neglect some of their duties, and who are not absolutely perfect. If *perfection* is the only proper test of a Christian state, I fear that we of the North might have our title to such a name called in question. But I will say all that I intend now to say on this subject, by adverting to two notable cases, which may at once serve to illustrate and to justify my assertions.

The celebrated and eminently pious John Newton, of London, was master of a slave-ship that went to Africa, several times, under his command. He tells us, that until the question was raised in England, by Wilberforce and others, he never once had a doubt in his mind of the lawfulness and propriety of the Guinea trade. To come nearer home ; who does not know that the immortal Edwards — immortal as much for his great piety as for his intellectual powers — left behind him in manuscript an Essay on the Slave-trade (probably still extant), in which he defended the trade with all his ability, on the same ground that Moses required the fugitive heathen slave to be detained, viz., on the ground that it would bring the perishing heathen within the reach of Christian influence. That his *logic*, in this case, would not well compare with that in some of his printed Treatises, I am fully satisfied. But the simple and proper question is: Did he intend any wrong ? Had he any motives of self-interest, which led him to argue as he did concerning the slave-trade ? Unhesitatingly we answer both questions in the *negative*.

May it not be, then, that there are some Christians in the South who are in the same plight, in which Newton and he were? For one, I say emphatically — Yes.

When will the time come, in which men shall cease to pronounce sweeping judgments of condemnation on their fellow men, without examining into their case, and giving them a fair and impartial hearing? I earnestly hope the day-break is approaching, although at present it seems to be receding. But — it is sometimes darkest just before day.

Thus far I have treated only of *Hebrews*, made slaves among the Hebrews, with the exception of one peculiar case of a foreign refugee. I now come, after exhibiting the full state of things among the Jews in respect to slaves of Hebrew origin, and the many modifications which Moses inserted in his laws to mollify the hardships and rigors of their condition, to consider THE CONDITION OF SLAVES, WHO WERE OF HEATHEN ORIGIN.

Here the abettors of the proposition, that all slavery is a *malum in se* and is to be ranked with murder and robbery, will find matter of serious difficulty. With not a few of the high-toned Abolitionists, I fear I shall bring Moses into much discredit, by quoting his enactment. But here it is, and it would not become me to offer an apology for him. Let him speak for himself:

Lev. 25: 44. Both thy bond-men, and thy bond-maids, which thou shalt have, *shall be* of the heathen that are round about you; of them shall ye buy bond-men and bond-maids. (45) Moreover, of the children of the strangers that do sojourn among you, of them shall ye buy, and of their families that *are* with you, which they begat in your land: and they shall be your possession. (46) And ye shall take them as an inheritance for your children after you, to inherit *them for* a possession, they shall be your bond-men for ever.

What now have we here? Simply and plainly an unlimited liberty to *purchase*, (not to steal), bond-men and bond-maids of the heathen around and out of Palestine, or of heathen dwelling within it. But when Moses says: " Ye *shall* buy bond-men and bond-maids," he is not to be understood as giving *command*, but permission. Our translators have here made the Fut. tense in Hebrew *imperative*, and as it were *jussive;* but every one acquainted with Hebrew knows, that the Fut. tense is very often *permissive*, i. e. it is used as a Subjunctive mode. However, on the liberty to buy, there

is no restraint whatever. When bought, slaves are declared to be heritable property — to belong to the children of the owners " to inherit them for a possession." Then follows the clause which rivets fast the tenure of the property : " *They shall be your bond-men* FOR EVER.". There is no seventh freedom-year here ; there is no jubilee liberation. These belonged to *Hebrew* slaves. The heathen bond-men are not put on a level with them. The tenure of them is perpetual, the tenure as of *heritable property.* " The middle wall of partition between Jews and Gentiles" was not yet broken down, but just erected. The time for declaring that there was one God and Father of the Jews and Gentiles, to whom all stood in the same common relation, was yet far distant.

There then stands the Mosaic statute, which was the perpetual law of the Jews. There it stands, not to be erased by the hand of the most zealous Abolitionist. He will probably think very ill of Moses, and not be very courteous toward me for venturing to quote him. However, if there is any blame here, it falls on the great Jewish legislator himself, and not on me. He, moreover, can afford to bear it.

In the name of all that is called *reasoning* now, in morals or religion, how is the ownership of slaves which heaven has given express leave to purchase, to be deemed a *crime* of the deepest dye — a *malum in se* — an offence to be classed with murder and trea-son ? Let those answer this question, who decide *a priori* what the Bible ought to speak, and then turn it over in order to see how they can make it speak what they wish. But there is no bending or twisting of Moses' words. There they are, so plain that "he who runneth may read." If Abolitionists are right in their position, then Moses is greatly in the wrong. More than this ; then has the God of the Hebrews sanctioned, with his express leave, the commission of a crime as great as that which he has forbidden in the sixth or seventh commandment. There is no retreat from this. The posi-tion of the Abolitionists plainly taxes high Heaven with misdemean-or, — with encouragement to commit one among the foulest of crimes.

What shall we say then ? Shall we consign Moses over to repro-bation ? Or are we to regard him as an *ignoramus*? One or the other, or both, follow from the reasoning and the premises of heated Abolitionists.

I have said that Moses needs no aid of mine in the way of apology. When he speaks the words of the God of the Hebrews, it is for us to listen, not to call in question. Yet it may be consistent with all the reverence due to him as the head of the ancient dispensation, to say a word that may help to open closed ears. Let what I have hinted, once and again, be here brought distinctly into view. The Jews were a separate, chosen, peculiar people. The Mosaic dispensation was a *preparatory* one, and not a complete, perfect, or permanent one. High was the wall of partition, while it lasted, between the Jews and heathen Gentiles. That slaves might be purchased of the latter, on conditions entirely different from the purchase of Hebrew servants, resulted, no doubt, from the fact, that the Jewish nation were to be trained up in such a way, as to consider the condition of the heathen as inferior to their own. In this way, contamination by familiar intercourse with them, on the terms of equality, was in some good measure prevented. To look on nations as fit to be enslaved, produced the same kind of feeling that the sight of African slaves now produces, in the minds of slave-owners, toward the people of Africa. Hence heathen marriages were forbidden as degrading to the Hebrews. The abominations of idolatry were such, both in respect to cruelty and pollution, that no intimacy was to be allowed. But the slaves purchased from the heathen were not likely to influence the religion of their masters. They were obliged, moreover, to be circumcised, and to keep the Jewish sabbath and feasts. Their *degraded state* prevented the danger of contagion from their heathen notions. The whole tenor of the Mosaic legislation on this subject seems to show, that the permission to purchase heathen slaves, was one of the means employed by Moses to render heathenism contemptible in the eyes of the Hebrews.

At all events, none can reason from the case of the Jews — the one favored, preëminent, secluded nation — to the case of men, who lived after the coming of Him, " who broke down the middle wall of partition between Jews and Gentiles," proclaimed one common God and Father of all; one common Redeemer and Sanctifier; that this God is no respecter of persons; and that he has " made of *one blood,* all the nations that dwell on the face of the earth " — I say none can now crave liberty to purchase slaves of the Gentiles or Jews, on the ground of Mosaic permission. He might as well insist on the liberty of polygamy and concubinage, both of which Moses allowed

—I cannot say *encouraged*, for evidently this is not the case. He allowed it for the same reason that he allowed divorce at the will of the husband. Our Saviour has told us what this reason was, viz. "The hardness of their hearts." The light of the gospel dissipates all these deeds done in claro-obscure light. All reasoning of this kind is null, if it be at variance with the spirit and precepts of the gospel; which is now our supreme law.

I have only one remark more to make, and then I go from Moses to his disciples in later periods. This is, that it is well worth. the labor of every serious man, who prizes his Bible, to look into the accounts we have, in books of Grecian and Roman antiquities, of the state of slavery among the two leading nations of the world, most renowned for learning and civilization. They gave to masters the power of life and death; they authorized them to scourge and imprison at pleasure; see Juvenal Sat. vi. 219. The master could put to death by crucifixion, at Rome; and this was the usual punishment. If the master of a family was slain at home, and the murderer could not be discovered, all his domestic slaves were liable to be put to death. Tacitus (Ann. xiv. 43) mentions a case, in which 400 slaves in one family were put to death under this law. Slaves were not supported among heathen nations, except by special kindness and comity; see Julius Pollux, Onomast., on the word παυσι-κάπη. They were rarely permitted to marry, or even to enter into that connection with a female, which the Romans called *contubernium*. Slaves, moreover, were debarred from all participation in the civil and religious festivals and rights of the citizens. Compare all this now with the laws of Moses. Does it not lie on the very face of his legislation, that he far outstripped all the legislators and sages of antiquity? How came he, issuing from Egypt the very hot-bed of polytheism and slavery, to know so much about the rights of men, and to do so much for the interests of humanity? There is but one satisfactory answer to these questions; and this is, that he had light from above.

But we come now to his followers. The first question which spontaneously presents itself here, is: Did subsequent prophets and teachers undertake to repeal or amend the laws of Moses?

The ready answer is in the *negative*. *Repeal* them they could not; for their commission and business was, to explain and enforce them. *Amend* them they could not; for they were already what

God designed they should be, under the Jewish dispensation. All they could do was to rectify mistaken views of them, correct popular errors, and urge the strict observance of all the Mosaic code.

Yet we are every day presented with examples of quotation, from the prophets or other sacred Hebrew writers, which, by the interpretation given them, are made to speak in direct contradiction to Moses. This practice has become so familiar and popular, that a multitude of Old Testament texts are pressed into the service of Abolitionists, which have no special bearing whatever on slaves or slavery. Oppression is forbidden; defrauding the laborer of his hire is forbidden; and (in a word) every injury which a man might do to his neighbor is prohibited. All this is put, by Abolitionists, under the category of denunciation against slavery. How little foundation this reasoning has, for the most part, we shall soon see. It becomes necessary to adduce examples, in order that the reader may fully understand what I am intending to say.

Of all the prophetic texts, I believe Is. 58: 6 has been the subject of appeal most frequent, and confident too. What says it? " Loose the bands of wickedness; undo the heavy burdens; let the oppressed go free; break every yoke." The prophet further enjoins, that they shall give bread to the hungry, house-shelter to poor wanderers, and clothing to the naked. He then adds: " *Hide not thyself from thine own flesh.*" And who then are they that are thus described? Plainly *fellow-countrymen, citizens of the same commonwealth, and kindred by blood.* Let the reader, if he doubts this interpretation of the expression *one's own flesh,* open his Bible at Gen. 29: 14 and 2 Sam. 5: 1. 19: 13, 14. Judg. 9: 2. It is clearly the oppressed and degraded *Hebrews,* then, of whom the prophet is speaking in this whole passage. It has no special relation to slaves at all, whether heathen or Jewish. Surely heathen slaves would not be called, by Isaiah, the " own flesh" of the Hebrews. Yet this passage is printed in staring capitals every day, as the sentence of an ultimate and supreme tribunal, which decides the cause of the Abolitionists in their favor.

For the sake of further illustration, let me revert once more to the respectable religious journal, to which I have made reference on p. 10 seq. above. The same keen sighted Ariel, who dates from Boston, and who has already been noticed (p. 10 above), after quoting some eight or ten names of subscribers to the commendation of

Mr. Webster's Speech, and putting Dr. Woods's name and mine in capitals, goes on to quote a sentence from Mr. Webster's reply to the communication he had received. The quotation is : " The day has come, when we should open our ears and our hearts to the advice of the great Father of his country," (Washington). Ariel then asks: " When will the day come, in which we will open our ears and hearts, to hear that Father who is in heaven ? " Forthwith he cites some five different texts from the Bible, and joins them into one mass, without any reference to the places where they may be found, just as if they all stood in juxta-position in the sacred volume. The first passage is Jer. 22: 13, which runs thus : " Wo unto him that buildeth his house by unrighteousness, and his chambers by wrong ; that useth his neighbor's service without wages, and giveth him not for his work." It seems not to have occurred to him, that it would be strange to hear the prophet speak of defrauding *slaves* of their *wages*. Did Moses ever expect or demand, that a slave should have *wages*? This inquiry would of itself set a considerate man to examining the case, in order to find out what such language means. But no; the text *sounds* all to Ariel's purpose, and so it is brought in. Unluckily however for him, the context (v. 11) shows us plainly, that the oppressive and tyrannical Shallum, the degenerate son of Josiah and heir of his throne, is the sole object of the denunciation. He built " large chambers, wide houses . . . ceiled with cedar and painted with vermillion," by exactions upon his subjects. The *woe*, therefore, is applicable to him, and (in this place) only to him.

Prov. 31: 8, 9 is next cited. It runs thus : " Open thy mouth for the dumb, in the cause of all such as are appointed to destruction. Open thy mouth, judge righteously, and plead the cause of the poor and needy." And who then are " the dumb, and those appointed to destruction?" The next verse shows that they are " the poor and needy," whose mouth has been stopped by some unrighteous and bribed judge, who refused to hear their plea, and so forced them to be dumb. And were *slaves* permitted to bring causes before the Hebrew courts ? Possibly our Ariel may think so ; but no one of course, who understands the matter, will be inclined to think with him.

The third passage is Ps. 82: 3, 4. " Do justice to the afflicted and needy. . . Rid them out of the hands of the wicked." The

Psalmist is addressing judges who act unjustly, (v. 2). The *wicked* here are such persons as bring the poor and needy into court, in order to enforce exactions upon them by bribing the corrupt judges. Were the slaves of the Hebrews, then, sued in court by their masters? I trust not; their masters needed no court but their own, and had a summary process within their own power.

The next appeal is to Jer. 34: 17. "Ye have not hearkened unto me, in proclaiming liberty, every one to his brother, and every man to his neighbor." The context (vs. 12—16) informs us, that the Jews of that day paid no regard to the liberation of Hebrew slaves, when the seventh or liberty-year had come. The masters still continued their bondage. Jeremiah threatens them, therefore, with divine judgments, on account of their perfidy to the law of Moses. But — not a word or syllable is here, about the bondage of *heathen* slaves.

The fifth and last appeal is to Isa. 16: 3. "Hide the outcasts; bewray not him that wandereth." And who are the *outcasts* and the *wanderer*? They are the fugitive daughters of Moab, who flee from the conquering invaders of their country, and seek safety in the land of Israel. The prophet presents them as addressing the Hebrew people, beseeching them, in the words quoted, to conceal them in a place of safety, and not to tell the pursuing enemy where they are, i. e. not to bewray them. This is all. But how this is to be put to the justification of concealing runaway slaves, or made into a command to aid and protect them, I have not sagacity enough to divine.

I should not refer to Ariel, who has thus exhibited his profound acquaintance with the Old Testament, if it were not, that he has merely given utterance to what is resounding on all sides. Such are the *conclusive* texts, which are every day appealed to with the most undoubting confidence, as speaking to the point which the Abolitionists are eager to establish. How much reason they have for such a confidence, has now been shown. Probably, however, it will be labor lost on most of them; for they seem very much prone to ignoring. Be it so; I still hope that the cautious and sober inquirer after scriptural truth, will at least be put on the alert, as to such quotations, and as to the interpretations which are given to them. As to Ariel himself — I know not who he is, and am glad that I do not, because I can now speak the more freely, without subjecting

myself to the imputation of personalities. I suppose, by his frequent appeals to the Scriptures, that he may be a minister of the Gospel. If so, I can only condole with his people, that they have not a more dicriminating guide, to lead them to a right knowledge of the meaning of the Scriptures. If the quotations above, and the construction put upon them, do not show him to be a mere sciolist in the knowledge of the Bible, it would be difficult to say what could exhibit proofs of such a predicament. I add only, that the last three texts above are printed in staring *capitals;* why, I know not, unless it be to proclaim to the world what a *capital* exegete he is.

I stop with these examples; for if I were to follow up and examine all the texts of Scripture which are every day abused in this manner, it would of itself require a little volume. I add here only a few brief reflections.

Let us now take a momentary *retrospect*. Where do the Hebrew Scriptures place and leave this whole matter? The answer is plain and undeniable. The Jews were permitted to purchase and hold slaves, who were of their own nation, i. e. native Hebrews. But this could be done only for *six years* at a time. When the seventh year came, each Hebrew was free ; and so at the jubilee-year they were all free, whether the six years had expired or not. Many privileges were granted to such persons, which were not usually granted among other nations. Moses made great advances in the matter of humane treatment. But the *unlawfulness* of such slavery, so modified, is a thing that Moses never once intimates.

But how was it with slaves purchased from the heathen? The Jews had *unlimited liberty* to purchase them, and to hold them as *heritable* property. There was no seventh year, and no jubilee-year, to them. Lev. 25: 44—46 has put this matter at rest, for all sober and honest inquirers. There it stands, (and even Abolitionists cannot abolish it), that the Jews might have slaves *ad libitum*.

Have the prophets contradicted this? Did the expounders and enforcers of Moses' laws occupy themselves with repealing and contradicting them? So the Abolitionists virtually conclude and declare, every day. I do not mean that they venture directly upon such assertions, but that they quote and apply the words of the prophets in such a way, as to set them in direct opposition to Moses. If they are not conscious of this, (as many of them do not seem to

be), or if they do not intend it, it is none the less a matter of fact —
a thing too plain to be overlooked. Why then should they vituperate, with so much unsparing violence, those who believe and maintain that Moses and the prophets have not contradicted each other,
but are in perfect concord?

One more suggestion, and I have done. It should be remembered,
that the Jewish commonwealth was a *theocracy*, or a *monarchy*, and
not a *democracy*. The people had not the right of electing rulers
and magistrates; nor any right to repeal or modify their laws.
These laws were ecclesiastico-political. They spread over all the
duties of religion and civil polity. They determined all the various
relations and relative duties of the community. What Moses had
ordained, no subsequent legislative Congress could repeal, or even
modify. If, then, he gave full permission to purchase and hold
slaves, (which he surely did), then, so long as the Jewish dispensation lasted, this permission could not be abrogated. God only could
change the Mosaic law; and therefore, if any Hebrew disliked slavery, he could only refrain from it himself, but could not demand of
his neighbors to refrain from it, much less denounce them if they did
not refrain.

Last of all; let it not be forgotten, that Moses was forty years at
the head of the Jewish nation, before he ventured on giving to
female slaves the same rights of freedom after six years, which the
Hebrew *bond-men* had. What do or can the zealous advocates of
immediate emancipation do with his example?

I have but one question more to ask, and I shall then leave this
part of our subject. This question is very simple and plain: Did
the God of the Hebrews give permission to them to commit a *malum
in se*? Did he give unlimited liberty to do that which is equivalent
to murder and adultery? To this point the matter comes. There
is no shunning the question. It will not do here, to allege that the
Hebrews were permitted to hold slaves, because they were an obsti-
nate and rebellious people. It is only in matters less strenuous than
this, (I mean such as were not *mala in se*), that any indulgence of
this kind could be granted. Crimes *mala in se* cannot be trans-
formed into *no crimes*, by heaven or earth. Slavery, therefore,
under the Jewish dispensation, by purchase from the heathen, was
not one of these crimes. The God of the Bible could never sanction
the commission of such. And yet, if Abolitionists are to be heard,

that God has sanctioned not only a positive evil, but one of the greatest of all crimes.

Enough for the Old Testament; come we now to the New.

§ 3. *The attitude of Slavery in the New Testament.*

We pass now from the ancient dispensation of the Law, which, in its very arrangements for worship and ritual, was confined to one nation, and was never designed to be a permanent and universal religion. The *moral* and *spiritual* part of it, however, has its basis in the relations of God to man, and of men to God and to each other. They are unrepealed, and irrepealable.

First of all, let us call to mind, that in our Saviour's time, the Jews were under a foreign power; whose appointed governor in Judea was a stern and jealous military commander. It needed a strong hand to keep the Jews under, and make them quiet; and such an one was laid upon them. They had no choice of officers, no appointment of magistrates, no means of vindicating their freedom and independence. It was in circumstances such as these, that our Saviour made his appearance among them as a religious teacher, and the head of a new dispensation. It is a deeply interesting question, when we ask: How did he, " who knew no sin," demean himself among the Hebrews with whom he lived and conversed?

There are a sufficient number of cases, by means of which we may see how carefully our Lord avoided all appearance of opposition to the government under which he lived, notwithstanding his full knowledge of the tyranny and injustice of the Roman governor. His disciples were applied to for tribute-money, and were asked, whether their Master paid tribute. The answer was, that he did. When Peter applied to him to know what he would do on a particular occasion, he asked him: " Of whom do the kings of the earth take custom or tribute? Of their own children, or of strangers? Peter saith to him: Of strangers. Jesus saith to him: Then are the children free." The meaning of this seems to be, that he, the Son of David and Son of God, as the sovereign of the Jews and of all men, might rightfully decline to give tribute to a heathen power. Still, he ordered Peter to take a fish, in whose mouth a piece of silver was found, and this was given to the exactor of tribute, both

for himself and for Peter; see Matt. 17: 24—27. In other words; he would set an example of being "subject to the powers that be," even when they required what he was not under obligation to give.

In Matt. 22: 16—21, is an account of a plot laid by the Herodians, to ensnare Jesus, by asking, whether it was lawful to give tribute to Cesar. They expected him, as a Jew, to answer the question in the negative; and then they meant to accuse him of sedition before the Roman governor. Or, if he should answer in the affirmative, then they meant to make him odious to the people, for his want of Hebrew patriotism. His answer was admirable: "Render unto Cesar the things that are Cesar's, and unto God the things that are God's." It is easy to see how utterly he frustrated their insidious designs. No wonder that the evangelist subjoins, that his enemies "marvelled, and left him and went their way." Yet he could, and doubtless did, regard the Roman sway over Judea, as merely the predominance of might over right.

When the Pharisees came to him, tempting him, and seeking to entangle him in a quarrel with the Jewish expounders of Moses' law, in regard to the matter of divorce at the will of the husband, he boldly answered at once, that Moses permitted this only " because of the hardness of their hearts; but that in the beginning it was not so." Mark 10: 2—9.

In John 8: 3 seq., we have an account of a woman taken in adultery, and brought to him by his enemies, in order that he might condemn her. He confounded them by saying: "He that is without sin among you, let him cast the first stone." One by one they all slunk away, and left the woman alone. "Jesus said to her: Where are those thine accusers? Hath no man condemned thee? She said: No man, Lord. He said to her: Neither do I condemn thee; go, and sin no more." The object of his enemies was, to lead him to meddle with a case which belonged to the civil and judicial tribunals. This he declined to do. And when he said: "Neither do I condemn thee," he meant merely that he did not undertake to give a *judicial* condemnation. Still, he left the woman no room to suppose that he was ignorant of her crime, or indifferent to it, for he said to her: " Go, and *sin no more.*"

Thus much in respect to the Saviour's cautious forbearing to intermeddle with, or oppose, the civil power. Had the civil juris-

diction been in his hands, or been assumed by him, there can be no doubt that every abuse of the then existing Jewish government would have been reformed. As the case was, he comprehended all his great design in one sentence, when he said to Pilate: "My kingdom is not of this world."

Let me now put some questions respecting the teaching and doctrines of Christ. In what part of the Gospels is there any record of his taking special cognizance of *slavery?* Where is even a direction to masters, or a declaration respecting the demeanor of slaves, to be found in them? I believe indeed, and I shall hereafter endeavor to show, that the Saviour uttered sentiments, which, in their ultimate effects, must abolish — totally and forever abolish — all slavery, except in cases of crime. But where did he intermeddle with the then existing relations between master and slave? Not a word is to be found in the Gospels indicative of such an interposition. And yet, there seems to have been great need of some interposition. It should be remembered, that the Roman power and laws were then dominant in Palestine. The Jews had only the power of controlling *religious* worship and rites. Of course, the cruel Roman laws were dominant there, which gave the power of life and death to the master of a slave. The Jews of that generation, also, were surely as bad as those whom Jeremiah denounced, for misusing their Hebrew servants. And yet, while almost every prevailing sin of the day is expressly and strongly denounced by the Saviour, he does not once touch on the abuses of slavery. Not even in his Sermon on the Mount, has he brought this matter into view. Why not? On the ground of the Abolitionists, who make it a *malum in se*, it is impossible to free him from the imputation of gross neglect and abandonment of duty, as a preacher of righteousness. I call now upon them to explain these facts. My statements they cannot deny. I ask then — I have a right to demand — some satisfactory explanation.

My own explanation (to which they doubtless will not accede) is, that Christ purposely and carefully abstained from meddling with those matters which belonged to the civil power. Slavery was one of these. An undertaking to dictate on this subject, would have subjected him to the accusation of being pragmatical in the affairs of the civil government. He would have been accused before the Roman governor. Nor was this all which influenced his course. He

doubtless felt, that slavery might be made a very tolerable condition, nay, even a blessing to such as were shiftless and helpless, in case of kind and gentle mastership. It was not like murder or robbery. It might therefore be tolerated for a while, rather than embroil himself and his disciples in a quarrel with the Jews and Romans. His policy differed, no doubt, from that of the immediate Emancipationists. He took care to utter truths and establish principles, which in their gradual influence and operation would banish slavery from the face of the earth; but he would leave the completion of the work to time, and to the slow but sure operation of the principles which he inculcated. He doubtless thought and said with Paul: " Art thou called, being a servant, care not for it." He, it would seem, believed that the sudden breaking up of the then existing frame-work of society, would have occasioned evils greater than slavery. He did not therefore issue any commands for immediate action, in respect to this matter.

His whole conduct, however, in regard to slavery, is every day *practically* called in question and condemned. Few venture indeed directly to attack him or to vilify his character. Still we have some bolder spirits, it would seem, in Boston, who do not scruple to cast contumely upon him, even in public assemblies; as some late scenes in New York testify. There are many, I fear, in our country, who do not think that any serious regard is to be paid to his teachings or his example, in respect to the matter before us. But still, there are many, I do hope and trust, who, although they seem never to have seriously reflected on this subject, may be induced to pause and examine, before they advance any farther in the career of violence.

Thus much in respect to Him who knew no sin; who spake as man never spake; and to whom was given all power in heaven and on earth. We come next to his apostles and disciples. Have they trodden in the steps of their Lord and Master?

Let us begin with Paul. The first passage which I shall quote, is Eph. 6: 5—9:

(5) Servants, be obedient to them that are your masters according to the flesh, with fear and trembling, in singleness of your heart, as unto Christ; (6) Not with eye-service, as men-pleasers; but as the servants of Christ, doing the will of God from the heart; (7) With good will doing service, as to the Lord, and not to men; (9) Knowing that whatsoever good thing any man doeth, the same shall he receive of the Lord, whether he be bond or free. (9) And, ye masters,

do the same things unto them, forbearing threatening : knowing that your Master also is in heaven; neither is there respect of persons with him.

Servants then, in the Apostle's view, are bound to be obedient — even with *fear and trembling*, i. e. with a high sense of reverence for their masters. *In singleness of heart*, i. e. with sincerity. *As unto Christ* strongly expresses the high sense of duty which they should cherish. The sixth verse has made this idea intense, by precluding all mere show or pretence of obedience, and requiring an obedience like that due to Christ, i. e. an obedience of the *heart* such as God requires, and because such service is the doing of God's will. Verse 6th requires all this to be done *with good will*, i. e. heartily, cheerfully, not grudgingly and with morose feelings. The 8th verse encourages such obedience by promise of reward. In the 9th, the *masters* are taught their duty. The clause *do the same things unto them* is somewhat obscure and difficult. *Same* as what? Surely not the same as the obedience required of the servant ; for this would make no sense. I do not see anything in the preceding context with which *same* may be compared, excepting the clause: " Whatsoever *good thing* any man doeth." The servants were to *do good* by ready, hearty, and cheerful obedience. The masters to *do good* to the servants, by kindness, lenity, and forbearance. So the next clause appears to explain it, *"forbearing threatening."* Paul would have servants rendered obedient by kindness which would win them, not by severe looks, threatening words, and a rod held over them. I believe there is many a master at the South, who honestly aims at obedience in this particular. Those who do not, should ponder well the last part of verse: " There is no respect of persons with God." In his sight, an obedient servant is as good as his master, even if his master is kind and gentle; unspeakably better, if he is severe and rigid in his exactions.

If such were Paul's injunctions, in respect to master and slave, how do the language and conduct of most Abolitionists accord with them? They do not scruple to tell the slave, that he owes no duty to his master, and that he ought to escape from his service if possible. They hesitate not to furnish him with all the means of escape, which are in their power. It has been publicly declared in this place, by one of the most distinguished orators of the anti-slavery party, that a servant would have as good a right to cut his master's

throat, if it were necessary in order to make his escape, as he would have to take away his life in defence of his own, when he was assailed with a deadly weapon. And this — all this — what is it, compared with Paul's view of the subject? And how is *conscience*, that mighty arbiter of all questions — how is it to be disposed of, on the present occasion? This question must be met; it must be met fairly and honorably. No evasion will answer the purpose. Nor is this passage to be *ignored*. Men, ministers of the gospel, politicians, Christians, are bound to meet it, face to face. If not, then let Paul be abjured. This is the only honest course, when we refuse to hearken to him. It is hypocrisy, if we profess to acknowledge him as an inspired teacher, and then flout at his doctrines, and ridicule and contemn those who inculcate obedience to him. The time has come when this matter is to be met *directly* and *honestly*. Tergiversation will not do. If Paul is cast off — that is one thing. An honest deist, if such a rarity can be found, might consistently ignore Paul. But this will not do for *Christians*. Many say, that to be the master of a slave, proves the want of Christianity, an unfitness for Christian fellowship. In what part of the New Testament is that found? On the other hand, one may with very much more reason say, that a refusal to obey Paul, an ignoring of what he has taught respecting slavery, and a vilification of all who plead for the duty of obeying him, is unspeakably stronger evidence of the want of Christian principle.

The Ephesian church was not the only one to whom Paul preached after the same tenor, in regard to slavery. To the Colossians (3: 22—25 and 4: 1) he says :

(22) Servants, obey in all things your masters according to the flesh; not with eye-service, as men-pleasers; but in singleness of heart, fearing God : (23) And whatsoever ye do, do it heartily, as to the Lord, and not unto men; (24) Knowing that of the Lord ye shall receive the reward of the inheritance : for ye serve the Lord Christ. (25) But he that doeth wrong, shall receive for the wrong which he has done : and there is no respect of persons. 4: 1, Masters, give unto your servants that which is just and equal : knowing that ye also have a Master in heaven.

As these words are mostly identical with those already commented on, much need not be said. One sentence only, in respect to *servants*, needs to be noticed. It is this, which is addressed to servants: " But he that doeth wrong, shall receive for the wrong which he hath

done; and there is no respect of persons." In other words: The servant who does the wrong of withholding hearty and cheerful obedience, shall be punished; for God will punish the wrong-doing slave, as well as the wrong-doing master. One other declaration respecting *masters,* needs some notice, specially since it has so often been misinterpreted and abused. It is this: "Masters, give to your servants what is just and equal." The shade of meaning in the original is not given by our translation. It stands thus in the Greek: "Show to your servants justice and equity," viz., in your dealings with them, and in your requirements of service from them. All excessive and rigorous demands are forbidden by this passage; and nothing more is meant by it. The Greek word ($\iota\sigma\acute{o}\tau\eta\tau\alpha$) means literally, when applicable to objects of sense, *equality.* But in the *moral* sense, (which is plainly the one here intended), it means *equity.* Many a time has this passage been produced to show, that masters are bound to make their servants equal to themselves, i. e. to make freemen of them. If so, then how could the Apostle insist, as he does in the preceding verses, on the sincere and thorough *obedience* of the servants to their masters? How could they be bound to *obedience,* after they became *freemen?* No — such an exegesis is *felo de se.* It is absolutely preposterous. On the other hand, that masters should be charged not to make unjust and inequitable demands on their servants, and that they should treat them with gentleness and lenity, was a doctrine worthy of him who preached it.

In 1 Tim. 6: 1—4, Paul has again given us his views very graphically :

(1) Let as many servants as are under the yoke count their own masters worthy of all honor, that the name of God and his doctrine be not blasphemed. (2) And they that have believing masters, let them not despise them, because they are brethren; but rather do them service, because they are faithful and beloved, partakers of the benefit. These things teach and exhort. (3) If any man teach otherwise, and consent not to wholesome words, even the words of our Lord Jesus Christ, and to the doctrine which is according to godliness, (4) He is proud, knowing nothing.

Here comes before us an injunction on servants to "count their masters as worthy of all honor," i. e. to treat them with high respect, and ready obedience. But why so? "In order that the name of God and his doctrine [the Gospel] be not blasphemed." In other words: 'If a course of conduct the opposite of this should be

followed, then heathen masters would revile the Gospel, on the ground that it taught their servants to be disrespectful and disobedient.' But further; in case master and servant are both Christians, the latter is not on this ground to claim a release from his obligations as a servant, i. e. because they are Christian brethren and one in Christ, it does not follow that their civil and social relations are changed. On the contrary, the masters are to be the more readily obeyed, because they are Christian brethren. To complete his directions, he enjoins it upon Timothy to teach these precepts, and to exhort those concerned to do their duty. But what if any man should teach *abolitionism* to the slaves, instead of Paul's doctrine? Then let him meditate awhile, and seriously too, on verses 3, 4.

Again in the epistle to Titus (2: 9, 10), we have the same sentiments repeated with new additions.

(9) Exhort servants to be obedient unto their own masters, and to please them well in all things; not answering again; (10) Not purloining, but shewing all good fidelity; that they may adorn the doctrine of God our Saviour in all things.

Here servants are required to " please their masters well in all things," i. e. to show a ready and cheerful obedience, "not answering again," i. e. not contradicting their masters, or gainsaying their commands. Here too they are specially forbidden to *purloin* anything; a vice to which, as we may naturally suppose, they would be very prone. But the Apostle requires *all good fidelity* of them. And what if they obey him? Why then " the doctrine of God our Saviour is *adorned* in all things," i. e. even by these acts of cheerful and faithful obedience in servants. Servants are told that they can *adorn* this doctrine as really and truly as their masters, or as nobles and princes and kings. Obedience to the gospel, in their difficult and trying condition, will add another jewel to the Redeemer's crown.

Thus far Paul. I need quote no more from him of the same kind as that already produced, although it might easily be done. But if what he has so many times repeated, is not worthy of credit, nothing would be added to it by the prolonged reiteration of the same sentiments.

Let us turn now to another apostle, the confidential friend and

disciple of Jesus, on whom was bestowed the honor of laying the first foundation stone in the new and glorious edifice of Christianity. Did *he* agree in sentiment with Paul? Let us hear him:

1 Pet. 2: 18, Servants, be subject to your masters with all fear; not only to the good and gentle, but also to the froward. (19) For this is thank-worthy, if a man for conscience toward God endure grief, suffering wrongfully. (20) For what glory is it, if, when ye be buffeted for your faults. ye shall take it patiently? but if, when ye do well, and suffer for it, ye take it patiently, this is acceptable with God. (21) For even hereunto were ye called: because Christ also suffered for us, leaving us an example, that ye should follow his steps.

What have we here? Paul again, through and through. Here, however, is one new circumstance added. Servants are to obey, readily and with reverence, " not only the good and gentle, but also the froward," ($\sigma\varkappa o\lambda io\varsigma$, *unjust, peevish*). Why should they obey even such masters? Peter tells us; for he says to servants, that " if when they do well and suffer for it, and still take it patiently, this is acceptable to God. Christ did well, and yet suffered on our account, thus leaving us an example." Yes — a god-like example it truly was. What greater honor for servants than to imitate him? Why did not Peter tell them: ' When your master deals hardly with you, it is your duty to run away?' We hear this among us, even preached from the pulpit, at present, almost every Sabbath, and proclaimed on all sides by journals called *Christian* or *religious*. Where do they get the right of wearing such a name? They certainly do not deserve it, for they have no proper claim to the honor, while they treat with scorn the idea of obeying Peter.

Thus much may suffice, in the way of *precept* from the New Testament, as to the duties of master and servant. Turn we now to that passage in Paul, whence our motto is taken. The whole passage (in 1 Cor. 7: 20—24) runs thus:

(20) Let every man abide in the same calling wherein he was called. (21) Art thou called being a servant? care not for it; but if thou mayest be made free, use it rather. (22) For he that is called in the Lord, being a servant, is the Lord's freeman: likewise also he that is called, being free, is Christ's servant. (23) Ye are bought with a price; be not ye the servants of men. (24) Brethren, let every man, wherein he is called, therein abide with God.

When Paul wrote this, he had just been discussing the question whether circumcision or uncircumcision was of any consequence.

He says it is of no consequence, so that no one need to pay the least attention to it. Then he utters what has just been quoted. The reader should note especially the general proposition in v. 20. Paul advises every one to remain in the same condition in which he was, when he became a Christian. If he was uncircumcised, let him not seek circumcision ; if circumcised, let him not seek uncircumcision. The full explanation of this last assertion would demand disclosures of some physical processes, not proper to be inserted here. But in passing from this matter to the consideration of slavery and freedom, Paul applies the same command or sentiment. He tells servants, that if they are called to be the Lord's freemen, while in a state of civil bondage, they need not have any solicitude about the matter — $\mu\acute{\eta}$ $\sigma o\iota$ $\mu\epsilon\lambda\acute{\epsilon}\tau o$, *do not care for it.* If I dared to degrade Paul's pure and sober diction, by translating it into our vulgar and colloquial dialect, I might exactly and faithfully give the real sentiment of the original thus : " Do not make a fuss about it." This is advice, which is not listened to ; as the eternal din and commotion on all sides, made too by those who are neither slaves nor in danger of becoming so, abundantly show. The advice is as completely ignored, as if it had never been uttered.

But we have not done with the passage. The next clause runs thus: $\dot{\alpha}\lambda\lambda'$ $\epsilon\dot{\iota}$ $\varkappa\alpha\dot{\iota}$ $\delta\acute{\upsilon}\nu\alpha\sigma\alpha\iota$ $\dot{\epsilon}\lambda\epsilon\acute{\upsilon}\theta\epsilon\rho o\varsigma$ $\gamma\epsilon\nu\acute{\epsilon}\sigma\theta\alpha\iota$, $\mu\tilde{\alpha}\lambda\lambda o\nu$ $\chi\rho\tilde{\eta}\sigma\alpha\iota$, lit. "but even if thou canst become free, rather make use of " . . . The reader of Greek will see that the verb $\chi\rho\tilde{\eta}\sigma\alpha\iota$, *make use of,* is left without a complement or Acc. case. Then comes the question, how are we to supply the deficiency? Or, (which is the same question), what does the ambiguous *it* of our translation mean? One and all of the native Greek commentators in the early ages, and many expositors in modern times, say that the word to be supplied is $\delta o\upsilon\lambda\epsilon\acute{\iota}\alpha$, i. e. *slavery, bondage.* The reason which they give for it is, that this is the only construction which can support the proposition which the apostle is aiming to establish, viz., 'Let every man abide *in statu quo.*' Even De Wette, (who for his high liberty-notions was banished from Germany), in his Commentary on the passage, seems plainly to accede to the force of this reasoning ; and with him many others have agreed. No man can look at the simple continuity of logic in the passage, without feeling that there is force in the appeal. But still I am not satisfied with this exegesis. We have full surely another and different noun, offered by the context, which we may

supply : "*If thou canst become* ἐλεύϑερος (*free*), *use* ἐλευϑερίᾳ (*freedom*) *the rather*," that is, rather than be a slave. This is certainly the most facile *philology*; although plainly not so congruent, at first sight, with the apostle's sentiment before and after this verse. What follows this? The apostle subjoins : "He who is called in the Lord, being a servant, is the Lord's *freeman*;" and therefore he need not be concerned about his civil bondage. So "he who is called, being a freeman, is the Lord's *servant*." In v. 24 Paul again recapitulates, at the close, the proposition with which he had begun : "Brethren, let every man wherein he is called, therein abide with God." The meaning of the last clause is: 'Let each one, whether a servant or freeman, continue in his calling, so demeaning himself as to preserve his alliance with God.' I am disposed to regard the clause : "But if thou mayest be free, use it rather," as a parenthesis thrown in *en passant*. So taken, it would serve to qualify the rest of the passage, respecting the general duty of servants. The opportunities to become free were not very frequent. The case of those who had not that opportunity, (by far the most frequent), was the one first to be provided for; and Paul has given his advice so as to make the servants contented and happy in their then present condition, if they will hearken to him. But to suppose that he gravely advises servants, to whom has been offered their freedom, rather to remain *slaves* than accept the offer, sounds strange, at least to our ears. So it did to Calvin's. I believe, however, that he was the first commentator of any note, who supplied ἐλευϑερίᾳ (*freedom*) after the verb χρῆσαι (*use, make use of*). This seems to have been the spontaneous prompting of the spirit of liberty, that beat high in his bosom. From him came the first germs of the Puritan principles in England, in respect to civil liberty. I cannot help agreeing with him here, although it is difficult to put aside the suggestions of the older commentators, which seem to rest upon the general course of thought, viz. "let each abide in his own calling." But I must on the whole think, that the clause which we are discussing is a parenthetic one, designed to make that case, in which a servant should have the opportunity of being free, an exception to the general rule. And I find in the ἀλλά (*but*, emphatic) a philological reason for this opinion. If we interpret with the ancients, we are obliged to translate ἀλλά εἰ καί by *even if*, a version which it will not well bear. In case, however, we make the *but* both disjunctive and *adversative*,

which is its proper meaning, then the interpretation which Calvin gave the passage, is a necessary one.

Only one verse remains for explanation: " Ye are bought with a price ; be ye not the servants of men." That this cannot refer to *civil* bondage is very plain ; because Paul had just advised servants to remain contented in that bondage, one case only excepted, viz. opportunity to become free. Plainly the verse in question refers to the preceding one, and was called forth by it. Verse 22 represents bond and free, who belong to Christ, as equal in a *spiritual* respect, and as equally regarded by him. What follows ? " Ye are bought with a price," i. e. you are all Christ's servants, because he has paid for you the price of his blood. And what naturally follows this ? Plainly, that because they belong to him and are his *spiritual* servants, they are not to serve, i. e. hearken to and obey, men who enjoin upon them to do anything which would forfeit their relation to him. " His *service* " [so named] " is perfect *freedom*." They must not lose this freedom, by following the dictates of any one, who requires them to commit sin, and forfeit his favor and their privileges. Such is the view of Chrysostom, Theophylact, and of De Wette ; and in this view I fully concur.

What have we, then, on the whole? Plainly this, viz., that servants are not to be anxious and uneasy and discontented, because they are servants. If they can easily and peaceably obtain their liberty, then they should accept the boon. But they are forbidden to be fractious, and querulous, and uneasy merely because they are in bondage. It should suffice, that they are the *Lord's freemen.*

Certainly this is not much like the advice or the conduct of most of the Abolitionists among us. They excite slaves in every possible way to change their condition, at all hazards and in all relations. They set the whole country in commotion, to accomplish this. Omnia — coelum, terra, miscentur ! They pour forth vituperation and contumely on every man who ventures to admonish them of the sentiments of Paul. And if the great apostle himself were to reappear on earth, and come now into the midst of us, and preach the doctrine contained in his Epistles, he would unquestionably incur the danger of being mobbed ; at all events, we should have a multitude of *indignation meetings* got up against him, like those which have recently appeared in the great metropolis of our country. Alas ! holy and blessed apostle, how little do such men know or partake of thy peaceful spirit !

Only one passage more from the New Testament do I design to recite, in respect to the matter before us. But this will come in better under our next category. The results of our New Testament investigation are few and simple. One spirit reigns throughout, viz., the spirit of peace, of good order, of ready obedience where obedience is due, and of obligation to contentment with our lot, unless some peaceful way of changing it can be devised. Not one word has Christ said, to annul the Mosaic law while it lasted. Neither Paul nor Peter have uttered one. Neither of these have said to Christian masters: "Instantly free your slaves." Yet they lived under Roman laws concerning slavery, which were rigid to the last degree. How is it explicable on any ground, when we view them as humane and benevolent teachers, and especially as having a divine commission — how is it possible that they should not have declared openly and explicitly against a *malum in se?* This problem the Abolitionists are bound to solve. It will do no good to dodge the question. It will come back again ; it will press itself upon them ; and they must give up the New Testament authority, or abandon the fiery course which they are pursuing. Common honesty and frankness demand this.

But we must not proceed to the next stage of our journey, before we have looked a moment at the civil condition and rights of the primitive Christians.

How entirely different were those from our own ! A representative — a republican government ? Who of all the ancients ever heard or dreamed of this ? Despotism, stern unrelenting despotism, under emperors, kings, viceroys, or their deputies, was in all countries the order of the day. What could a freeman in Palestine do, in our Saviour's time, toward altering or amending the government ? Nothing at all. A mere calling in question its measures was treasonable. Any intermeddling with civil relations or rights, would have been deemed sedition. *Slavery* was one of these relations. The supreme power of the land allowed and regulated this ; and only such a power had or claimed the right. Hence, if Christ, or Paul, or Peter, had said to masters: 'Set your slaves immediately free,' the answer would have been : 'Who made thee a ruler or a judge over us ? Cease to preach this sedition, or we will immediately bring you before the magistrate.' There were always masters enough ready to say and do this : and then, what was to become

of the infant cause of Christianity? The whole power of the Roman government would have been brought down upon it, to crush it in the bud, and never to suffer it again to rise up. Paul, Peter, and other disciples, thought it best to wait with patience for the greater prevalence of Christianity, and its more matured state, before they urged obligations on masters to free their servants. "The acceptable year of the Lord" had not yet fully arrived.

It is on this ground that I explain the silence of the New Testament, in respect to breaking the bonds of servants. I shall, however, endeavor hereafter to show, in due time, that there is enough in the New Testament forever to burst these bonds asunder. But it lies in a kind of occult state. I mean that it is so expressed, as not to excite the jealousies of heathen masters. It comes to us in simple moral costume, like the ordinary precepts of morality and piety. In this shape it excited no alarm. It roused up no jealousies. But — simple and seemingly enveloped as it is, it amply covers, after all, the whole ground in question. This was regarded by Christ and his apostles, as the safer and better way of leading men successfully to understand and to do their ultimate duty. But I shall leave the consideration of this *most important* part of the subject before us, to another and subsequent part of these Remarks.

§ 4. *The influence which Christian Principles should have on our minds, in relation to Conscience, and to the agitated questions of the day.*

There is yet one more passage to be quoted from Paul, which has a direct bearing on the most fiercely agitated question of the day. That question may therefore be put first in order, that we may complete, in a continuous course, our examination of those parts of the New Testament, which have a direct and explicit bearing upon the matter of slavery.

There is a clause in the Constitution of the United States, which has given occasion, perhaps more than anything else, to the excitement which now exists. Art. IV. § 3 says: "No person *held to service or labor* in one State, under the laws thereof, escaping into another, shall, in consequence of any law or regulation therein, be discharged from such service or labor, *but shall be delivered up*, on claim of the party to whom such service or labor may be due."

My first question is: 'Had the compacting States a *right* to make such an agreement?

Why not? Observe that the word *slave* or *slavery* is not once named. The Declaration of Independence had, eleven years before, published to the world the following noble sentiments, worthy of Christians, of patriots, and of advocates for the rights of man, viz., "We hold these truths to be SELF-EVIDENT; that ALL MEN are created EQUAL; that they are endowed by their Creator with certain UNALIENABLE rights; and that among these are life, LIBERTY, and the pursuit of happiness." There these words stand, emblazoned in light which even the blind can see, and never — never to be erased or obscured. After such a declaration before heaven and earth, without one dissenting voice, how could the immortal men, whose names are appended to that Declaration, publish to the world in their Constitution of government, that they fully admitted in practice what they had solemnly denied in principle? How could they say: We authorize the practical denial of equality and liberty, and hold, that the right to them of a part of the community is *not* inalienable? How would the despotisms of the old world have pointed the finger of scorn, at the palpable disagreement between the Declaration of Independence, and the Constitution of the United States!

It will be seen, by a moment's reflection, that the appearance of such a contradiction is in some measure saved, by the softened language employed, viz., *held to service or labor*. Nor is this all. As the matter now is, the article in question does not apply to slaves only, but equally to all other persons lawfully bound to service or labor, to apprentices, to men under special contract, to all in such a predicament, whether free men or slaves. All this shows the dominant feeling, at the South as well as the North, on the subject of slavery at that time, viz., the feeling óf repugnance. Moreover, it is a correct index of the then dominant state of feeling, as we shall see further on.

But allowing all that has now been said, still, could not the States mutually bind themselves to the compact before us? Surely they could. We must begin the examination of this subject by calling to mind, that each State was, and still is, a *sovereignty* within itself. Then, it was absolutely and entirely so; but now, in a more modified and limited manner, since it has assigned over a part of its sovereignty-rights to the General Government. Each State, then,

could, and can now, form laws for itself regulating all rights of property or of citizenship. It could admit any particular class of men to the privileges of citizenship, or it could exclude them. It could decide what rights one man had, or could have, over another, as to demanding *service* or *labor*. The compact in the Constitution merely declares, that the decisions of each State, shall be respected and admitted as valid by all the others.

This being all plain and certain, it follows, that when men held to service or labor by the laws of one State fly to another, the property or service can be reclaimed and enforced, as by law belonging to the citizens of that State from which the fugitives came. The words of the compact are : " Shall be delivered up, on claim of the party to whom such labor or service is due." Now what does or can this mean ? First, it certainly does not mean, that obstacles can lawfully be thrown in the way of such claimants. Secondly, it implies of course, that the *claim* to the fugitive should both be valid and be duly established. Thirdly, the article has, very unfortunately, omitted all special direction or provision, as to the manner of establishing said claim, and all definition of *delivering up*. This language of itself would seem to imply, that the State to which the fugitive comes, has him, some how or other, in its *custody ;* if not, how can he be *delivered up* ? It cannot well mean, that the State to which the fugitive has come, is bound at once to take *active* measures for the purpose of accomplishing a restoration ; for how can this be done, except the right of the claim be first established by the owner? But where and how is this to be done? The question of property, or right of ownership, in the case before us, is one which can be lawfully decided nowhere but in the State to which the fugitive belongs. The ownership is wholly dependent on the laws of the State where the owner lives, not on the laws of another State. And in accordance with this view of the matter, has the decision of the Supreme Court of the United States been made. All that is to be done by another State, to which the fugitive comes, is, not to throw any obstacle in the way of reclamation. To Congress, and to that body alone, it belongs to legislate, as to the mode of carrying into execution the compact which has been made. They have thus far failed to do it effectually ; and now the evil resulting from this failure has become very great, and the difficulty of legislation at present is immensely augmented.

It is plainly beyond the power of any one State to say to another: 'You shall not claim this or that as property.' It may feel that other States have wrongly and injuriously decided this question. It may have a *moral* or *admonitory* Christian duty to perform toward her; but on the ground of national law, how can one sovereignty usurp authority to decide for another, in regard to their internal relations and concerns?

What now has the constitutional compact actually done? It has simply bound all States to acknowledge as property, that which any particular State, acting within its own jurisdiction has decided to be property, and of course it forbids all detaining of it, and commands deliverance of it, wherever the claim is properly made out.

What participation then have we of the North, in any injustice that may be done to the slave, in making him property? Not the least in the world. We have simply agreed, to deliver up to the inhabitant of another State, that to which he has a claim sanctioned by the law of that State. We have merely renounced, in an express manner, a jurisdiction which in fact we never had, and cannot have. The renunciation removes all ground of doubt or dispute. What is the harm or sin of this? And what is the use of assuming a jurisdiction, which never did, and never can, belong to us?

'But the States have no right to make men property,' it is said. That may be so, I reply; and considered merely in a Christian light, I believe it to be true. But what right now has Massachusetts to decide for Virginia, on such a question? Virginia may do wrong, (I fear she is so doing), but Virginia is not under our supervision or jurisdiction; nor are we, in any degree, accountable or responsible for her errors or sins! The simple question before us is: " Whether full faith and credit shall be given in each State, to the acts of another?" The Constitution declares, that this shall be done, Art. IV. § 1. Shall we now obey it? Every magistrate in the land takes an oath to obey it. How can he do this, if he does not mean to keep his oath?

But we are told, that there is a higher law than the Constitution, the law of heaven written on our hearts and consciences; and that we are to follow that law. Nay, it is not only proclaimed in some of our journals, that there is a higher law than the Constitution, but men are called upon, both in those journals and in the pulpit, to disobey the Constitution. Conscience, it is said, has decided, and

rightly decided that the Constitution should be disobeyed. But how? Why? Can my private conscience prescribe to Virginia how she shall regulate her laws of property? Can my conscience decide, that sovereignties are not to be left to their own sense of duty? I do not see how. I may think that Virginia, for example, does a moral wrong by her slavery laws; but it is clearly no political wrong done to others. The matter belongs to her alone; not to her neighbors.

But let us here look into this matter a little farther about *conscience*, and its alleged rights. Is the conscience in question a *Christian* conscience? There are, as we well know, all sorts of consciences, very diverse and even opposite; but I am asking now for a *Christian* conscience. To every such conscience I would say: Come along with me now to another conference with Paul. I insist upon it that you shall not decline.

What did Paul do at Rome? A slave of Philemon, at Colosse, ran away and came to Rome. There he was converted to Christianity under Paul's preaching. The apostle was so pleased with him, that he was desirous to retain him as a friend and a helper. Did he tell the slave that he had a right, nay that it was his duty, to keep away from his master, and stay with him? Not at all. He sent back Onesimus, the slave, to his master (Phil. v. 12), and he tells the master, that he could not venture to retain Onesimus without knowing whether he would consent, v. 14. "Perhaps," says the apostle, "he departed for a season, that thou shouldst *receive him forever.*" He then expresses his ardent desire, that Onesimus may be treated with great kindness, and as a *Christian* ought to be treated.

What now have we here? Paul, sending back a *Christian* servant, who had run away, to his *Christian* master; and this even when Paul had such an estimation of the servant, that he much desired to keep him as a helper, while he himself was in bonds for the gospel's sake. Yet he would not continue to do this; although it was so desirable to him. He enjoins it upon Onesimus to return to his master *forever.* This last phrase has reference to the fact, that Paul supposed that the sense of Christian obligation, which was now entertained by Onesimus, would prevent him from ever repeating his offence. And all this too, when Philemon, being an active and zealous Christian, would in a moment have submitted to any command of Paul respecting Onesimus. Why then did Paul send him

back? There is only one answer to be given, viz. that Paul's Christian *conscience* would not permit him to injure the vested rights of Philemon. He could not think of keeping the servant, even to minister as a friend to his own necessities while in prison. Paul's conscience, then, like his doctrines, was very different from that of the Abolitionists. Paul's conscience *sent back* the fugitive slave; theirs *encourages him to run away*, and then protects him in the misdeed, yea justifies, applauds, glorifies him, as a noble, independent fellow. The conscience of Paul sends back the fugitive, without any obligation at all on the ground of compact; theirs encourages and protects his escape in the face of the most solemn national compact. And all this for *conscience'* sake! That may be the case, perhaps; for conscience, when misled by rashness and heated party-spirit and enthusiasm, can turn into any shape whatever. Paul himself says, that he acted *conscientiously*, when he persecuted Christians unto death, and laid waste the church of God, Acts 23: 1. Ignatius Loyola had a conscience. Xavier had more conscience than most men ever had. Yet the conscience of one founded the tribunal of the Inquisition in Europe, and of the other, the same in Asia. St. Dominic had a conscience. Mary queen of England had a strong conscience. So had James the Second, and even Jeffries made noisy claims to one. The Hindoo mother, who throws her child into the Ganges, has a conscience. The hangers of witches among us surely had a conscience. The Quaker men and women, who went about the streets, and into public assemblies, *in puris naturalibus*, had a deal of conscience. And so, when judgment is kept down, and passion set up, and men become in their own conceit wiser than all others, they can manufacture a conscience into any possible convenient shape.

Such would seem to be the fashion of many consciences at present. Conscience bids them violate the Constitution of our country. There is a higher law than this, say they. But I ask: Who has discovered and determined such a law? The honest answer would be, their own passions and prejudices. It is a conscience wholly *subjective*. Talk of conscience in violating a solemn compact? Of a conscience which condemns the conduct of Paul, when acting under divine guidance? Must we trust in a conscience which plainly accuses him of either having no conscience, or else a very bad one? Can we respect a conscience, which puts the broad seal of disgrace and infamy on those immortal men and patriots, who formed our

Constitution, and who in all our States accepted and approved of it? And where now has *conscience* been, these 60 years past? What sort of men have adorned our legislative halls, our pulpits, our churches? Men, it would seem, who did not understand even the first rudiments of religion, or of civil freedom and the rights of man. Has conscience slept profoundly so long in the fathers, and now have their children become all at once "wiser than Daniel," and discovered what poor, grovelling, half-witted men their fathers were? All this is wonderful to me, I must confess. I am astounded at the rapid railroad progress of new discovery. If there was not a syllable in all the Bible respecting slavery and the manner of treating it, it could not be treated with more neglect than it now is, in regard to this subject.

Look at some of the demonstrations. To recur to that respectable religious journal, which I have more than once made the subject of remark; not long since, a writer in this journal, who has chosen a star for his signature, came out and told the public, that the article in the Constitution about delivering up fugitive slaves, is a breach of heaven's higher law; that his conscience forbids him to obey it; and he tells his countrymen that he shall disobey it. If now a *star* cannot give better light than this, methinks it will but "disastrous twilight shed." I hailed with joy the rising of that star above the horizon, and heartily welcomed it. I did fondly hope, that in its progress it would come and stand over Bethlehem, "the place where the young child was." I watched with interest its movement. Alas! how was I grieved by the last observation I had of it, during the recent anniversaries at New York — grieved to find that it had passed on from Bethlehem, and was hovering over the land of the Philistines. May its return to Bethlehem be speedy! A noble star it may be if it does not wander from its orbit.

The question: Where was conscience, when our Constitution was formed and approved, brings to my mind another question, viz. What would those exalted and noble patriots have thought, or how would they have felt, could they have been called forth from their graves, and have made their appearance in the midst of the two different anti-slavery meetings recently held at New York? I could not help thinking more particularly on one great and good man, who took an active part in all the formative process of our general government, and by his skill and wisdom saved our new settlements from

the horrors of Indian aggression. Every one will of course know, that I speak of the illustrious JOHN JAY. What if his portrait had been hanging in the hall where the Anti-slavery Society recently met, under the presiding auspices of his descendant? Would it not have brought to every mind, the recollection of what the earl of Chatham said, when addressing a descendant (then in the house of Commons) of a noble ancestor, whose picture was in full view? His words were: " From the tapestry which adorns these walls, the immortal ancestor looks down, and frowns upon his degenerate offspring." I must except, in my application of this declaration, the last two words. They should not be applied to such a man as the Hon. William Jay. But I may say: Would not his immortal ancestor have looked down with a mixture of sorrow and of frowning, on a descendant who could exhort his countrymen to disregard and trample under foot the Constitution which his father had so signally helped to establish; and who could pour out an unrestrained torrent of vituperation upon Mr. Webster, who has taken up the Constitution where Mr. Jay's ancestor left it, and stood ever since in the place of the latter as its defender and expounder? How would that agitated and frowning face, moreover, have gathered blackness, when the presiding officer of that meeting went on to say, that Mr. Webster had not made his Speech from any conviction of sentiment, but because the cotton merchants and manufacturers of Boston demanded such views to be maintained, and these gentry had of course given it their approbation. This — all this — of such a man as Mr. Webster ! And all this too — of the Boston gentlemen who commended Mr. Webster's Speech ! To one who knows them as well as I do, this is absolutely shocking. At all events, it is ungentlemanly; it is passionate; and what is more than all — it is *absolutely false.* To see the Hon. W. Jay, presiding over such a meeting, and opening it with declarations which degrade and villify his illustrious ancestor, and hold him up to contempt, forces from one the spontaneous exclamation: *O quantum mutatus ab illo!*

And what did the meeting do, who were thus presided over? They passed a long string of resolutions, which are about as good proof of the matters which they assert, as the resolve of Anacharsis Cloots was, which he proposed to the National Assembly of France, and which ran thus: " Resolved, That there is no God; reason dethrones equally the King of heaven and the kings of earth." Here is a specimen of the Hon. Mr. Jay's Society-doings:

Resolved, That DANIEL WEBSTER, by his disregard of early professions, his treachery to Humanity and Freedom, and his servility to the Slave power, has forfeited the respect and confidence of his constituents and country.

Resolved, That we view with astonishment the abetting of the Massachusetts' Senator in his apostasy and inhumanity by men eminent in the learned professions, in literature and in the church; and that the CHAIN recently presented to him in this city is a fit emblem of the spirit of those who bestowed and him who received it.

"Angels and ministers of grace defend us!" my respected Friends, and Fellow-signers of the Letter of Commendation. What are we to do, since we are placed in such an awful predicament? Where hide our heads, after thus endorsing "apostasy, inhumanity, and treachery?" Yet — wait a moment. From whom, now, does such a bill of attainder proceed? is a question, after all, which we, my Fellow Signers, may stop to ask, before we flee for terror into exile. Yes, *from whom?* From a Secretary of the Society, who is every way worthy of such resolutions as these; from one who has long since lost caste among all respectable and sober men, and exhibits marked signs of preferring to reign in a certain bad place, rather than serve in a certain good one. Courage, then, my Friends! Possibly we may yet survive and weather the storm. If so, then,

"Blow winds, and crack your cheeks!"

I now take my leave of this *American and Foreign Anti-Slavery Society,* and turn for one moment to the so-named *American Anti-Slavery Society,* the father and prototype of all the others, presided over by the Genius of slander, vituperation, and profaneness. But what have I to say to them? Nothing; if possible, less than nothing. They may be assured that their words pass by as the idle wind, and are as little regarded.

But — I am making too long an episode. Let us go back to the *conscience,* which bids us to violate our solemn compact contained in the Constitution; that conscience, which stigmatizes Paul as a coward and a *pro-slavery* man. I will present one more, and only one, exhibition of it, and then gladly make my retreat.

A member of Congress from Ohio, not long since, declared in his place in the House of Representatives, that "he would sooner *hang a man for sending back a runaway slave,* than for any other crime whatever." Alas! for the apostle Paul, if he were now among us

and should fall into his clutches. This noble martyr received from the Jews, five times, forty stripes save one; thrice was he beaten with cudgel-rods; once was he stoned; thrice he suffered shipwreck, besides enduring an infinitude of other vexations and annoyances; but now he would fare worse still. He would be " hanged by the neck, until he was dead," in the very midst of a *Christian* land! The gentleman who said these decent things, has once been virtually sent home to his constituents, for his disgraceful conduct in the House to which he belongs. It were well for the country and our good name and peace, if he were sent for good to an Insane Hospital, where he properly belongs.

Enough, and more than enough, of such revolting exhibitions. They cover our land with disgrace, and hold us up to the nations as an object of derision, or of exultation in the hope of our speedy dissolution. Well may the advocates of despotism forbode evil, when defiance to sacred compacts stalks abroad, and waves over our land the sceptre of truce-breaking and of disunion. They must needs forebode evil, when the precepts of Paul are ignored, and the blessed apostle is threatened with the halter, for sending back a fugitive slave. America has already become a by-word among the nations, for her *repudiation* of contracts and of laws. But a short time ago, a friend of mine made the tour of Europe, and was everywhere pointed at with the finger of scorn, where he staid long enough to become known; and often was he saluted by strangers, with *Monsieur Repudiation!* in France, and *Repudiations Bürger!* in Germany. Who does not feel shame mantling his cheek, when he reads this? AMERICAN — a name which was once an open passport to the best society in Europe — and not long since, none so poor as to do it reverence. We are now but just beginning to recover from that disgraceful plight, when we are again threatened with the old sin on a higher scale.

We have done for the present with a truce-breaking, Paul-reproaching *conscience*. Let us look once more at the requisitions of the Constitution in regard to fugitive slaves, and inquire into the expedients proposed, in order to remedy the evil of disobedience to these requisitions.

A brief history of this matter seems necessary to a right understanding of it. In 1793, Congress passed a general law, empowering all State magistrates regularly appointed by States, to adjudicate

cases of claim on fugitive slaves, and give certificates of transmission back to the State from which they had fled. For fifty years this was acquiesced in, and no serious disturbance or complaint arose. But in 1842, in the case of Prigg vs. the State of Pennsylvania, the Supreme Court of the United States decided, that the subject of fugitive slaves belonged exclusively to Congress, and no State Legislature had any right to intermeddle with it. The very next year, the State of Massachusetts, (stung to the quick by the South Carolina law, which imprisons colored Massachusetts' freemen without judge or jury, and without the allegation of any crime subjects them to the loss of liberty, money, and time, and all this without providing for any remuneration), passed a law, that none of their magistrates should henceforth take cognizance of fugitive slaves, and that no sheriff or under officer of the like kind should aid in arresting, detaining, or imprisoning any fugitive, and that no prison in the commonwealth should be used in aid of those who claimed fugitive slaves. A fine not exceeding $1,000, or imprisonment not exceeding one year, was the penalty affixed to disobedience.

In 1847, Pennsylvania followed suit, by enacting laws equally severe and prohibitory. Ohio also, by a series of laws at different times, threw obstacles in the way of recovering fugitives, which were equally difficult to be surmounted. Some other Northern States have done the like; while some have coöperated with the Constitution, in aiding the restoration of fugitives. The Supreme Court of the United States, in the case of Prigg, declared, that where State magistrates are not *prohibited* by a State Legislature, *they may lawfully exercise the power of giving certificates for the return and restoration of fugitives*, under the United States law of 1793. But a considerable number of States having enacted such a prohibition, no remedy was left for the master but that of going before the United States District Court, which would often be attended with more delay and expense than the slave was worth.

Thus stood these matters, until what is called MASON'S BILL was proposed. That is now under discussion, and bids fair to rouse up the whole country, and greatly increase the difficulties of the case. That bill makes not only the United States District Court a tribunal for the trial of cases under discussion, but empowers all commissioners or clerks of said court, and all postmasters or officers of the customs, *residing* or *being* within any State, to try and adjudi-

cate all cases of this nature, and to issue a mandate of restoration. This bill moreover declares, that every person obstructing or hindering the claimant in his rescue, or assisting the fugitive (knowing him to be such) to escape, shall forfeit $1,000, be imprisoned one year, and be subject to a private action besides, on the part of the master, for damages sustained.

This bill, which at the North has been familiarly named a *Bill of Abominations*, if it is not quite worthy of so reproachful a name, contains several things which, as I must believe, would lead to abominations. The apprehension that Mr. Webster had pledged himself to support this, in his speech before the Senate, has been, perhaps more than everything else, the occasion of the unparalleled excitement that now exists. As his speech was first published, there was apparently no alternative but to believe such an apprehension to be well grounded. For myself, I always supposed, from the first, that there must be some mistake, which had been overlooked; for I felt well assured in my own mind, that Mr. Webster would never go the lengths of that bill. It is now fully apparent, that I had good grounds for my suspicion. From one of our most respectable papers, I have taken the following *correction*, premising that it comes from the hand of a man who might claim a near place to Mr. Webster in respect to talent, integrity, and patriotism. The correction runs thus:

" The truth is, that no person who heard the speech, and no candid man who has read it, ever supposed Mr. Webster to have pledged himself to the particular and specific amendments suggested by Mr. Mason. A change of location of one single word, which probably stands as it now does, by the reporter's misapprehension or mistake, removes all the ground for the elaborate and fulminating censure of the Atlas. The speech now reads thus :— ' My friend at the head of the Judiciary Committee has a bill on the subject, now before the Senate, with some amendments to it, which I propose to support, with all its provisions, to the fullest extent.' Change the position of the word *which*, and the sentence would read thus :— ' My friend at the head of the Judiciary Committee has a bill on the subject, now before the Senate, which, with some amendments to it, I propose to support, with all its provisions, to the fullest extent.' It has been again and again repeated, but is entirely false, that Mr. Webster named Mason's amendments as those which he intended to support.

" We are authorized to state two things; first — That Mr. Webster did not revise this portion of his speech, with any view to examine its exact accuracy of phrase; and, second — That Mr. Webster, at the time of the delivery of the speech, *had in his desk three emendatory sections*, prepared under consultation with

a high judicial authority, who has had more to do with these questions than any judge in the country, and one of which sections provides expressly for the right of trial by jury. These sections had already been suggested to members of the Senate most interested in the question, with an intimation that it was intended to propose them, when the bill should regularly come up for consideration.

" The writer of this article heard every word of the speech, and understood it to be exactly what it would be with the change of the word as before mentioned."

I merely add, that Mr. Webster himself has personally assured me, that his speech was in accordance with the correction here made, and that he has now in his desk the amendments to which the corrector refers. Thus much in respect to this matter, which has given so great offence—an offence however which, as the matter stood at first before the public, was not without some apparent ground. The worst of the case is, that now, since this mistake has been corrected, the high-toned Free-Soil and Abolition papers still continue to *ignore* the correction. Is this justice? Is this candor?

As to the bill itself, it plainly contains some preposterous provisions. Any postmaster or collector whatever, whether *resident* in the State, or merely *being* in it, (such is its language), may take cognizance of a fugitive's case, and give orders for his remittance. All this, too, without any trial whatever, or any other proof than oral testimony, or an affidavit made before any one who can administer an oath. What hinders the master, then, coming from Virginia or any other slave State, from bringing a Southern *postmaster* with him; and, when they have come to Massachusetts, it may surely be said of such postmaster, that he *is* (*being*) in the State, where the fugitive is. What hinders a slave-catcher from the South from coming to Massachusetts with his confederate postmaster, and laying hold of any free colored man here, so as to bring him to trial before the said postmaster, or before one of our own bribed postmasters, and then to take the man off to a slave-market? Do you say: 'There must be proof of bondage?' Very well; but is not the manufacture of the proof required, completely within the power of that slave-catcher? A man who can engage in such a business, is capable of forging any proof that he needs.

What now shall we say to all this? Is the great question of man's natural right—that *inalienable right*, as our Declaration of Independence calls it—is such a question as that to be put in the power of every and any postmaster? God forbid, that such trifling

as this with a question of such moment to a fellow being, should ever be allowed, or thought of! No! NEVER, NEVER! No, Mr. Mason. We of the New England States believe that negroes are *men ;* we believe that " GOD HAS MADE OF ONE BLOOD *all the nations that dwell upon the earth."* And if they are *men*, the question of freedom cannot be so lightly dealt with as your bill proposes. The next that we should hear of would be, that some Bruin is on our soil, with a postmaster confederate, and hurrying off our freemen to the land of slavery. This will not do. We cannot incur the danger of such a thing.

And then the *penalty* for interposing in the execution of such a summary process — it looks very much like the expression of passionate severity. It is immeasurably beyond the demerit of the alleged crime ; although, I must confess, that the law of Massachusetts of 1843 stands pretty well by the side of it in this respect, and has even less ground of excuse ; for the United States Court have decided, that State-officers *may adjudge* such cases of fugitives, and Massachusetts has said they shall not. At all events, however, any such law as Mr. Mason's, is a perfect *felo de se.* It would operate just as the bloody code did in England, when there were some 220 or 230 crimes punishable with death. No jury could at last be found to convict. Even murderers escaped, through the horror which the juries had of legal cruelty. So would it be here. Could I see Mr. Mason, I should feel disposed to say to him : ' Sir, I regard you as an honorable and a talented man ; but you must pardon me for saying, that you do not know the North ; above all, you do not know New England. Why Sir, it would be as perfect a piece of Quixotism as was ever exhibited, to bring the offenders which you describe, before (for example) a Massachusetts jury. A juryman who, for such an alleged crime as you describe, should vote to inflict the penalty you propose, would lose caste as a New Englander for ever. Your bill is, therefore, a bill of *impossibilities.* It utterly overlooks the state of things and of society at the North. We are born here with an instinctive aversion to slavery ; we believe that it is not doing to others, what we would that others should do to us. And to fine a man in the enormous sum of $1,000, to imprison him moreover for a year, and then subject him to a civil action besides, for injury done to the master — and to do all this merely because of an interference which humanity pleads for, although the law con-

demns it, is Turkish justice, not American — at any rate not New England justice. Such a bill is as much out of question here, as a bill of *Prudhomme's* making would be, which defines *property* as meaning *crime.'*

I do not, be it noted, justify *interference.* It is against our United States Court, and the law of international justice. And as to all the efforts to lead men to trample that Court under foot, I have given my honest opinion at full length above. But the remedy against such a breach of solemn compact, must be sought in a more just and feasible way than that which Mr. Mason proposes.

The Committee of Compromise, in the Senate, have given to the country a much more acceptable proposal than Mr. Mason's. I insert their own words here, so that all may read and interpret for themselves.

" The owner of a fugitive from service or labor is, when practicable, to carry with him to the State in which the person is found, a record, from a competent tribunal, adjudicating the facts of elopement and slavery, with a general description of the fugitive. This record, properly attested and certified under the official seal of the court, being taken to the State where the person owing service or labor is found, is to be, held competent and sufficient evidence of the facts which had been adjudicated, and will leave nothing more to be done than to identify the fugitive.

" The committee conceive that a trial by jury in a State where a fugitive from service or labor is recaptured, would be a virtual denial of justice to the claimant of such fugitive, and would be tantamount to a positive refusal to execute the provisions of the Constitution ; the same objections do not apply to such a trial in the State from which he fled. In the slave-holding States, full justice is administered, with entire fairness and impartiality, in cases of all actions for freedom. The person claiming his freedom is allowed to sue in *forma pauperis;* counsel is assigned him ; time is allowed him to collect his witnesses, and to attend the sessions of the court ; and his claimant is placed under bond and security, or is divested of the possession during the progress of the trial, to insure the enjoyment of these privileges ; and if there be any leaning on the part of courts and juries, it is always on the side of the claimant for freedom.

" In deference to the feelings and prejudices which prevail in the non-slave-holding States, the committee propose such a trial in the State from which the fugitive fled, in all cases where he declares to the officer giving the certificate for his return, that he has a right to his freedom. Accordingly, the committee have prepared, and report herewith two sections, which they recommend should be incorporated in the fugitive bill pending in the Senate. According to these sections, the claimant is placed under bond, and required to return the fugitive to that county in the State from which he fled, and there to take him before a competent tribunal, and allow him to assert and establish his freedom if he can, affording to him for that purpose all needful facilities."

I do not well see, what more can be done, at present. Here is no trifling with *postmaster* jurisdiction. If this measure is carried, and faithfully obeyed, I do not perceive what more we can demand or expect at the North, so long as the Article in the Constitution remains, respecting the restoration of fugitives. This looks like sobriety, and political justice, to say the least. For one, I should be satisfied to leave the matter in this position, and give it a fair trial. I do not know what Mr. Webster's proposed amendments were ; but I should suppose he might be satisfied with the present proposed Committee Bill.

To the position of our honored Legislature, in their recent Resolves, viz. that the case of the fugitive shall be tried " by jury in the State where the claim is made," I am unable, highly as I respect their motives, to yield my assent. How is it in all other like cases? If a fugitive from justice in Massachusetts goes to New Jersey, and he is there demanded by our Governor, must he have a jury-trial there of New Jersey men, before they can agree to give him up? Not at all. What right have they to try the case of a Massachusetts criminal? None, by any law or usage whatever. And are not fugitive slaves from the South, criminals in the eyes of Southern law? Most plainly they are. And have not the Southern States a right to determine for themselves, what and whom they may regard as criminal? Plainly they have. And when a fugitive slave comes here, who has done what their laws regard as criminal, have they not the right to have him remanded, and tried by a jury or court of their own States respectively? I must confess this seems a very plain case to me; so plain, that I cannot in any way accord with the resolve of our honorable Legislature. I cannot think that it is based on the common principles of public law, and certainly not on those of *Jus Gentium.* Besides, what the Committee have stated in their Report above, is no doubt accordant with what would be matter of fact, in case such trials were allowed.

I have done with this subject. The brief result, as it strikes my own mind, is, that the CONSTITUTION in respect to fugitives held to service or labor MUST BE OBEYED. It is useless to talk about *conscience* as setting it aside. It is an imputation on the men who framed our government. It is holding them up to the world as having neither conscience nor humanity. Under the regulations proposed by the Compromise Committee, I can at present, see no

formidable difficulties in the way of obedience. I do not believe, moreover, that *pains* and *penalties* for the aiding of fugitive slaves, if they are severe, can ever be inflicted. In my own view, such persons should be suable before the United States District Court, by the owner of the fugitives; and he should be entitled, in case illegal interference could be proved, to the full value of the slave, and to his expenses in the prosecution. Beyond this, I do not believe penalty can practically be inflicted.

I am happy to be able to introduce a paragraph here, from a late Speech in the House of Representatives by one of Massachusetts' most distinguished sons, who adorns private life as much by his virtues, as he does the Halls of Legislation by his soul-stirring eloquence. I refer to the Hon. R. C. Winthrop of Boston. He is speaking of the allegation made on all sides, of a law superior to the Constitution of the United States, and of the right which *conscience* has to trample on the requisition made by that Constitution. These are his words:

"I recognize, indeed, a Power above all human law makers, and a Code above all earthly constitutions! And whenever I perceive a clear conflict of jurisdiction and authority between the Constitution of my country and the laws of my God, my course is clear. I shall resign my office, whatever it may be, and renounce all connection with public service of any sort. Never, never, sir, will I put myself under the necessity of calling upon God to witness my promise to support a Constitution, any part of which I consider to be inconsistent with his commands.

"But it is a libel upon the Constitution of the United States — and what is worse, sir, it is a libel upon the great and good men who framed, adopted, and ratified it; it is a libel upon Washington and Franklin, and Hamilton and Madison, upon John Adams, and John Jay, and Rufus King; it is a libel upon them all, and upon the whole American people of 1789 who sustained them in their noble work, and upon all who, from that time to this, generation after generation, in any capacity, National, Municipal, or State, have lifted their hands to Heaven, in attestation of their allegiance to the Government of their country — it is a gross libel upon every one of them, to assert or insinuate that there is any such inconsistency! Let us not do such dishonor to the Fathers of the Republic, and the Framers of the Constitution. It is a favorite policy, I know, of some of the ultraists in my own part of the country, to stigmatize the Constitution of the United States as a *pro-slavery contract.* I deny it, sir. I hold, on the other hand, that it is a *pro-liberty* compact — the most effective pro-liberty compact which the world has ever seen, Magna Charta not excepted — and one which every friend to liberty — human liberty, or political liberty —ought steadfastly to maintain and support."

Noble, independent, and manly words are these. I cannot read them without thanking God, that we have men in Massachusetts who can speak as he does, and who are so well fitted to breast the tempest, and keep steadily on the rounds of a leader in the corps which constitutes the life-guard of the Temple of Liberty.

By the side of this extract from the Speech of this fearless champion of moral and civil obligation to honor and fulfil solemn engagements, mutually made by neighboring nations once virtually independent, I will place another paragraph, extracted from a late Speech of Mr. Ashmun, one of our Massachusetts Representatives. After reciting the article in the Constitution which demands the restoration of fugitive servants, he thus proceeds:

" This reads very plainly, and admits of no doubt, but, that so far as fugitive slaves are concerned, the Constitution fully recognizes the right to reclaim them from within the limits of the free States. It is in the Constitution which we have all sworn to support, and which I hope we all mean to support; and I have no mental reservation excluding any of its clauses from the sanction of that oath. It is too late now to complain that such a provision is there. Our fathers who formed that entire instrument, placed it there, and left it to us as an inheritance; and nothing but an amendment of the Constitution, or a violation of our oaths, can tear it out. And, however much we may abhor slavery, there is no way for honorable, honest — nay — conscientious men, who desire to live under our laws and our Constitution, but to abide by it in its spirit."

Par nobile Fratrum! I say, from the bottom of my heart. These are the sentiments which are to save our country if it be saved; and the good old Bay State has much reason to thank God that she has men in our national Council, who can stand up in the face of tumult and obloquy, and speak in behalf of covenant-keeping and of the Constitution. And what now becomes of the assertion, echoed and re-echoed the world around, that Mr. Webster stands *alone* in Massachusetts in defending the requisitions of our national Constitution? *Alone*, forsooth, with such men at his side! *Alone*, when in the single city where he resides and its near precincts, that List of names was made out and proffered to him, which has so excited the jealousy and the indignation of impassioned agitators!

I come next to the so long agitated *Wilmot Proviso*, as it is called. Mr. Winthrop has shown, that this Proviso originated some years ago, from his own hand, when the Oregon question was agitated, and that it was originated at first only for a particular purpose, which is

exhibited and explained in his Speech. But it is no matter whence it originated. The *principle itself*, asserted by the Proviso, viz. that the freemen of the North ought not voluntarily to consent in any way to the *extension* of slavery, is one to which I give my most unlimited and hearty assent. But the expediency of applying this Proviso to new Territories, and even the legal power to do so, is a matter that may be called in question. For such an opinion, I am bound to assign some good reason, and I will endeavor to meet my obligation.

I begin with the original relations of the United States to any *territorial* domain. The United States possess the land. On this new settlers cluster, not within the bounds of any specific State, and of course not belonging to any State. Then who and what are they? Are they our *subjects*, as *citizens*? A citizen must belong to a State; and unless he does, he can of course claim none of the specific privileges of a citizen. More than this; unless he does belong to some State, then what is our right of legislation over him? He occupies our land; but this does not confer on him the privileges, nor subject him to any of the onerous and peculiar duties, of a *citizen*. The United States have never ventured to tax Territories. They have never ventured even to legislate for them. The most which they have claimed, is the right to appoint a kind of guardian-governor. A Territory must have its Representatives, or Senate, or both, *within itself*, and *from its own population*. So it always has been, and so it must be, unless we assume the attitude of European despots, who govern Colonies by a military governor and a military *regime*. We, who guarantee a *republican* government to all under our supervision, cannot assume this attitude.

In permitting Territories to have their own self-appointed legislatures, we renounce the power of internal, civil and domestic control. But is not the question of *slavery*, a matter under their own control? The United States never meddle with that question; at least they never should, for the Supreme Court have decided, that they have no right to meddle with it. Whence then comes our right to say, either that a Territory shall, or shall not, admit slavery? If there be any such power, how are we to exercise it? We commit internal and domestic relations to a legislature of the Territory's own choosing. Whence comes our right then to exempt slavery from their own control; and above all, how do we possess a *right*, since our Supreme Court have decided, that we cannot legislate at all in Congress on the matter of civil and domestic relations?

But suppose that as *guardians pro tempore* we dictate to the Territories on this subject to-day, and say to them: " You shall have no slaves." To-morrow, they ask for admission as *States,* and we of course agree to it in case they are republican, and thus constitute them *States.* As *States,* all control about the matter of slavery of course is completely and entirely and *exclusively* in their hands. All feel obliged to concede this. They then convene their Legislature, the very next week. That Legislature has adequate power, and exclusively the only right or power, to say : " We admit the privilege of holding slaves." Is there any power on earth to gainsay or oppose them ? None whatever. They are a *State;* they are *sovereign* to all intents and purposes, as to their internal polity. No *previous* legislation, on our part, can in the least degree affect them.

These I take to be principles plain and incontrovertible. But if so, what is the *use* or *good* of Wilmot Provisos ? None, or at the most, none excepting that for a few days, or months, we may prevent slavery ; although our right or power to do that is, as has already been shown, certainly very questionable. Besides, were they to make a *compact* with us as a mere Territory, (there is no *political corporation* as yet to make one), were they to submit to our dictation of a compact, it would not be binding at all on them as a *State.* But as we have no right to make or demand such a compact, of course it is null ; and as they have no acknowledged corporation to make it, it is therefore doubly null. It must be true of both, that *quod non habet, non dat.*

Suppose now we put the old simple question — *Cui bono?* What is the answer ? No one, I think can be at a loss to give it. It is *profitable* to nobody ; for the state of things in which we have even any show of right to dictate, is one which can usually last but a few months; or at most not more than two or three years. And is this worth a four years' contention, and half of the time of Congress during most of that period, and of late the whole ? If there was ever a case on earth of *much ado about nothing,* this is plainly one of them. Four years' dispute about a Proviso, which, if made, is *ipso facto* annulled by a Territory's becoming a *State!* I would we could stop with saying that it is a mere *good for nothing;* but we cannot. It has occasioned much embittered feeling. It has called into activity all the heated passions of both parties. It has threatened the Union itself. It has alienated the North and South, perhaps irreconcila-

bly. And all this — for what? Why for the assertion of a right to dictate, where none existed; or even if the right be admitted, it can continue to be valid only a few months, or a year or two at most.

I must confess, that to me, a humble, quiet country-dweller, who never descended into the arena of political controversy, there has seldom a greater nonsense ever presented itself to my notice, than this said Proviso. It is impossible to defend it, on any stable grounds of *Jus Gentium* which a republic admits.

Mr. Winthrop declares himself ready to drop the matter. He never originated it for the purpose to which it is now applied. He meant only to defeat a wrong measure in respect to Oregon. Mr. Ashmun declares that he will not insist upon it. Mr. Webster says that it does no good; that it amounts to nothing in the end; and that it is not worth quarrelling about, at all adventures. The North gives up nothing that belongs to it, in abandoning it; it can gain nothing by insisting on it, even if it should carry the point. It can decide nothing for the State yet to come into being. Is it not, then, in reality *much ado about nothing?* And if so, why should another word ever be spoken in favor of urging it?

Is Mr. Webster now to be *ostracised,* because he looks on the whole affair as merely jumping up and down, without an inch of progress? He may be; but — shame on those who are concerned in such an *ostracism!*

The next great stumbling block is the admission of new States, carved out of Texas. When the act for receiving Texas as a State in our Union was passed, a clause was inserted in the resolutions (ch. 3, § 2) of the following tenor:

" New States, of convenient size, not exceeding four in number, in addition to said State of Texas, and having sufficient population, may hereafter, by the consent of said State, be formed out of the territory thereof, which shall be entitled to admission under the provisions of the Federal Constitution. And such States as may be formed out of that portion of said territory lying south of thirty-six degrees thirty minutes north latitude, commonly known as the Missouri Compromise line, shall be admitted into the Union with or without slavery, as the people of each State asking admission may desire; and in such State or States as shall be formed out of said territory north of said Missouri Compromise line, slavery or involuntary servitude (except for crime) shall be prohibited."

Several things lie on the face of this clause. (1) Four additional States *may* be made hereafter, by the leave of Texas. (2) That if

any portion of Texas has a sufficient number of inhabitants and presents a republican Constitution, (these are the *provisions* of the Federal Constitution), " it *shall be entitled* to admission." If the State to be formed, is north of 36° 30′, it must exclude slavery; if south of that line, it may admit or reject. The first of these prescriptions is a matter of *coram non judice*. There is not, until the State is actually formed, any party in that section of country, which is a corporate body, and entitled to make such a contract. If the Territory has declared for independence, then Congress has no right to legislate for it. If it has not, then there is only one legitimate party for the making of the compact, and it is of course null. But leapnig over all this, (and a large leap it must be), then comes up again the old *cui bono* question. The very day that the new State is made, it can tread under foot all the provisos that Congress can put upon it, when they respect things over which they have no lawful power to legislate. That they have none, in the present case, is just as clear, as that a State has the only sovereign right to decide on the civil and social relations of its citizens, and that Congress have no right to legislate where the Constitution has not conferred this right upon them.

So then, a new State or States north of 36° 30′ have, and can have, no *legal* obstacles in the way of admitting slavery. But as to the new States south of the line, the sovereign dispensers of civil and social rights at Washington have graciously permitted them to do as they please, about the matter of slavery. Well however might these new States say: We thank you, most benevolent gentlemen, for your consent that we should do as we please; but we expect to do so, and have a right to do so, whether you consent or refuse.

All this now lies on the very face of this whole matter. And yet Mr. Webster is assailed with the cry of *apostasy*, and with the charge of deserting New England, or Northern principles, and catering for the votes of the South. But what, let us coolly inquire, what has he done? He has said: 'We are bound on our part, to abide by our solemn compact with a sovereign State. We are obliged to admit four new States from Texas, if they come with the requisite qualifications to ask for such a privilege. Be they formed how or where they may, if Texas consent, and they have a sufficient number of inhabitants, and present us with a republican Constitution, we have

solemnly pledged the faith of the nation to admit them.' Is this now not a matter of fact? Is there not such a pledge? Can we recall it? Can we violate it? Yes, we can — but never again could the United States lift up its face among the nations, if the faith of solemn treaties or compacts is to be violated. Mr. Webster's crime is, that he insists upon it, we shall be a covenant-keeping nation. Is he to be treated with insult and contumely for this? Heaven forbid!

I am aware of the game that has been played by some ingenious and talented men with the words *may* and *shall* in the resolution of Congress above exhibited. There is no good foundation, however, for playing this game with success. The first *may* confers power and liberty for any desired new State formed out of Texas, to ask for admission *ad libitum*, provided they come under and comply with the usual conditions of States to be admitted. The next declaration is, that coming in this way, "they *shall be* entitled to admission." In other words, the United States positively pledge themselves to receive and admit a new State, on the conditions expressed. These conditions being complied with, where is the *may* that some ingenious gentlemen find in this resolution of Congress? The *may* depends on Texas and the new State; the *shall* belongs to us, when a new State is desired, and is in a constitutional state of preparation for admission.

I am not a little surprised at a paragraph in the Hon. Horace Mann's Letter to his constituents, in respect to the matter before us. He makes it out, that Mr. Webster could not tell how much four, minus one or two, would amount to. This is capital. What next? Mr. Webster, says he, has declared that we have guarantied that four slave States shall come in; and that such as are south of 36° 30' may come in as slave States. But Mr. Webster's words are so placed by Mr. Mann, as to convey a meaning quite different from that which Mr. Webster intended. Mr. Webster had not the least intention of saying, that the United States shall, on their part, make four new States at all adventures; but that if Texas and said new States agree, and the proper qualifications are exhibited, then the United States have bound themselves to admit new States to the number of four. Mr. Mann wishes to know where the *four* slavery States are to be found, when one or more free States have been formed north of the line in question. In this way he endeavors to

show, that Mr. Webster cannot count four minus one, and also that he has made five new States instead of four. In answer to all this special pleading, and (if I had not a high regard for Mr. Mann I should be tempted to say) trickery of argumentation, it needs only to be said, that neither Mr. Mann, nor any body else, can at present tell where the four new States will be first formed, and first apply for admission. The highest probability is, that they will all be south of the line in question. There is no temptation to go north. The land on the south is beyond measure more promising and capable of cultivation. Suppose now that the four States which first seek admission are all south of 36° 30, then of course the United States have pledged themselves to admit them; and this done, Texas can ask for no more, under the old compact. If another State comes in north of the line, it must be on the ground of a new contract and new liberty of admission. Where then is the absurdity of Mr. Webster's statement? Nowhere. The only expression in it which can give occasion to doubt, is, that " the guaranty is, that new States shall be made out of it" [Texas], which might be interpreted as meaning, that the United States have pledged themselves to cause so many to be made. But the context removes every doubt as to his real meaning.

Of Mr. Mann I can never speak but with respect. The glowing ardor and eloquence of his compositions, the intense love of liberty with which he is inspired, the humanity by which he is actuated, the fine scholar-like accomplishments which he exhibits, all command my respect and admiration. Whether his judgment and prudence are equal to his ardor and his energy, is another question, which is not before my tribunal. He professes the strongest regard and the highest respect for Mr. Webster, and avows solemnly his intention to treat him in a manner that corresponds with this avowal. I doubt not that he was sincere in making his avowal. But his impetuosity led him astray, after all. After repeating Mr. Webster's words, that he regarded the compact with Texas as solemn and binding, as binding as any legislation could make it, he goes on to say, that " he knows no form of statement, nor process of reasoning, which can make it more clear, that this [viz., what Mr. Webster had said] is an *absolute and wanton surrender* of the rights of the North, and of the rights of humanity." And this — from a man who professes the highest respect and regard for Mr. Webster!

Et tu, Brute?

Such are the envenomed arrows, which this new Free-Soilism and Abolitionism stores up in the quivers of its advocates. I know of no better exhibition or proof of the tendency of the spirit which it engenders, than is to be seen in the cases of such men as Judge Jay and the Hon. Mr. Mann. It can furnish gentlemen, scholars, men of cultivated minds and hitherto blameless lives, with the whole stores of annoyance that exist in the magazine of vituperation and calumny, and prompt them to the active appropriation of these stores. This is enough to make any sober quiet man pause, and ask whether such is "the armor of truth and of God."

No, Mr. Mann; "a *wanton surrender* of the rights of the North," is not to be said of Daniel Webster. Swords would leap, if it were lawful and necessary, from hundreds of thousands of scabbards, to defend him against such an assault. The Athenians, led on by Themistocles, may ostracise Aristides to-day; but soon — soon I trust, will they recall him from his banishment, and give him the honors due.

I pass over declarations of Mr. Mann in his letter, which, if not equally ungentlemanly and violent, are at least as little capable of sober defence. Mr. Mann is evidently exposed to many a thrust, for his paralogisms, and his colored and imperfect statement of facts. I leave those things, however, to others, who know how to espy the places which Mr. Mann's shield does not protect. I am proud of him as a man, a scholar, an orator, and a lover of liberty; but when he plays a game like the present, I can only say, that I heartily wish him a more creditable employment. It is eclipsing a sun, that might do something much better than 'shed disastrous twilight over half the nation.'

I do not suppose, that such a gentleman as I take Mr. Mann to be, designed to compliment himself, when he speaks of 'his words being as cool as the iron of the telegraph wire, while his mind is like the lightning which darts through it.' I am ready to acknowledge that there is not a little of the *electric* fire in Mr. Mann. But I cannot overlook the fact, that this fire can sometimes scorch and smite down, as well as be the swift messenger of tidings. If Mr. Mann has performed something of the last office of electricity, he has also given us a pretty fair specimen of the first.

A few questions more, and I quit the subject of new States out of Texas. To begin back; Has Mr. Webster ever voted for or advo-

cated the admission of Texas? No. How then did shè come in? By the recreant votes in the Senate of two Free Soilers, now riding on the whirlwind and directing the storm of disunion. Did **Mr.** Webster vote in any case whatever, for the extension of slavery, or of slave Territory? NEVER. Will he so vote? NEVER, so long as he is *Daniel Webster*. Did he ever vote to make a war of conquest, in order to extend slavery-ground? NEVER. Did he not contend to the last against Texas union and Texas contracts? *He surely did.* Has he lost any of his feeling of repugnance and opposition to slavery? NOT IN THE LEAST. It has been strengthened by all that he has lately seen and heard; and with good reason. Is there a man in the United States Senate, who has a more deep, solid, lasting, unchangeable dislike of slavery and all its attendant evils? NOT ONE. There are many men who make much more noise about it, and labor to turn the world upside down in order to throw it off; but not one of such, I venture to say, has so deep, steadfast, and immutable a dislike to it and disapprobation of it, as he.

What has he done, then? He has declared, that bitter as the task may be, to allow of new slavery States, still he must lift up his hand to carry solemn contracts into execution, to keep the plighted faith of this nation. There is — there can be no *repudiating* of such contracts. Even a *bad* bargain must be kept. If not, who after this can ever trust to the faith or honor of this nation?

And is Mr. Webster to be maligned, and vituperated, and thrust out of the confidence of his fellow-citizens, because he will not vote to violate solemn compacts? If this must be done, such a day awaits this nation, as no politician has yet imagined, and no prophet yet foretold. I will never believe that such a day is coming, upon the State in which are to be found Fanueil Hall, and Bunker Hill, and Concord, and Lexington, and the descendants of the men who immortalized themselves there. If such a day must dawn on us, for one I would say, rather than gaze upon it : " Hung be the heavens with black!" Patriotism, integrity, firmness, sound judgment, lofty soul-thrilling eloquence, may thenceforth despair of finding their reward among us.

In looking back over the ground that we have travelled, I cannot suppress my tribute of gratitude to our worthy President, for having taken the ground of *laissez faire* toward our newly forming States

and Territories. There is where prudence, *Jus Gentium*, and a proper regard to our new neighbors, call on him to leave the matter. I do not expect that the man, who coolly declined the condescending offer of Santa Anna, when surrounded by more than triple the number of soldiers under the American commander — the offer, that in case the latter would capitulate, liberal terms should be granted him, and much blood be saved — I do not expect such a man to quit his position, and bow to the dictates of partizan zeal. God bless him in his steadfastness, and bless the wise and prudent policy which he is pursuing!

With all becoming respect for our honored and honorable Congress of the United States, I would say, that I hope they will forgive a humble, but from the heart faithful, adherent to the Union, when he says, from the deep conviction of his soul, that he is much afraid, lest the spirit of legislating about everything and every body is becoming dangerously prevalent in our national Councils. It can do nothing but mischief. Such *Proviso* articles, as the whole country have been quarrelling about these four years, never can promote the public good. Much, very much, better is our President's plan of " *letting well enough alone.*"

One word on the use that has been made of Mr. Webster's declaration, that the Wilmot Proviso was useless, because the God of nature has so formed California, New Mexico, etc., that slavery is impossible ; and that we need not reënact the laws of Heaven. The Hon. Mr. Chase, of Ohio, and our own Hon. H. Mann, have both so harped on this string, as to make it produce no very melodious sounds. They know of only two powers, and these, as they say, are God and the devil. The laws, then, which are not made under the guidance of the former, must of course be made under the influence of the latter ;— and then they ask : What sort of laws will these be ? I might answer, perhaps, that they would be somewhat like the Wilmot Proviso law ; but I fear these gentlemen might begin to talk about demanding *satisfaction.* Quitting this, then — for I am a man of peace — let me ask, in my turn, whether there is any example of a numerous and prosperous slave population, in any country, like these *quondam* Mexican States ? Has a man any inducement to keep slaves, where he cannot raise and export enough to pay for their maintenance ? The countries in question are neither sugar nor cotton countries. Tobacco may be

raised, perhaps, in the valleys; but what has become of Virginia tobacco-lands? Can slavery ever thrive, where slaves cost more than they can earn? I know of no such thing. It has not been, and it cannot be; at least it never can be from choice.

Of what use is it, then, to occupy four sessions of Congress with the discussion of Provisos, which are directed against what can never happen? Suppose now that Congress should say, by their solemn legislation: We will protect and foster New Mexico and other neighboring Territories, provided they will let water run down hill, and iron be hard, and lead sink in water, and trees and grass grow. Another additional resolve declares, that the new Territories shall permit the sun to rise, and shall not stop the moon, or the tides, in their course. Would not all this be *sapient* legislation? Just about as sapient, in my view, as the Wilmot Proviso. How much time, and money, and effort has this absolute nihility cost our country already! A mere chase after a Jack-o'-lantern is it; and, like such wandering meteors, it has led us, in the chase after it, chin-deep into the swamp. And now, while we are floundering about there, some are beginning to open their eyes at last, and perceive, by the time that they are merely half-opened, that they have been pursuing a veritable phantom. But others still say: "We would make *assurance* doubly *sure* by the Wilmot Proviso." *Assurance* of what? There is not a man in the Union, in his sober senses, but knows, that if Congress vote that Proviso to-day, and to-morrow admit a Territory to become a State, that State has, from that hour, full power and right to convene the next day, and adopt slavery if it pleases. What is it, then, which is *assured*?

It is impossible to justify clamorous demand for such a perfect non-entity as said Proviso. Is it not a matter of grave, yea of alarming and melancholy reflection, that the North and South are to be put at irreconcilable variance and hatred, the Union severed, and the country deluged in blood, for such a pragmatic and trifling affair as this? My hope is in God, that our national Council will soon view this thing in its proper light, and adopt the wise and salutary policy of our chief magistrate.

Enough, and more than enough, of this Proviso. I have only a few words more to say, on points touching Mr. Webster, and then I shall pass on to another part of my task.

From Dan to Beersheba the changes have been rung, on Mr.

Webster's omission in his speech, of the topic of the South Carolina law, which imprisons our colored freemen of the North ; and especially his failing to say a word about the treatment which our honored, and well deserving to be honored, fellow citizen (Mr. Hoar) received, in his mission to the aggressive State in question. A few facts I will state in relation to this matter, and then dismiss it.

Mr. Webster had selected *ten* different topics for his speech, and had written out his thoughts to the amount of from two to three sheets on each topic. He carried with him to the Senate Chamber only a little scrap of paper, on which was merely a notation of each head. He was called on to speak, before he expected to do so; for others had the right of speaking before him, and he did not suppose they would choose to relinquish that right. Thus situated, and having no time for immediate preparation to commence speaking, he was constrained to begin speaking forthwith, and to go on continuously, (a thing which he did not anticipate or intend). In this pressure, his eye passed over *two* of the ten topics marked for discussion ; the one was the South Carolina proceedings, the other the territorial boundaries of California. The former he inserted in his Speech as corrected for the press; the other was reserved for another occasion.

As to inserting, in his printed speech, matter which was not delivered in the Hall of Legislation ; this is a thing done every day of the Congressional Session, and no one thinks of objecting to it. But that this affair should be put to the account of Mr. Webster, as an intended bait for the South, and as a currying of favor in that quarter by keeping *silence* in respect to what was disagreeable to their feelings, and thus making a *sub rosa* bid for the Presidency — all this is passing strange to me. *Silence*, forsooth! Silence? when Mr. Webster forthwith published to South and North too, the very thing that he is accused of ignoring. And has it come to this, that such a shallow trick (which is even no trick) at electioneering, which none but a half-witted sciolist in politics could ever play — that such a piece of *wonderful* cunning, can be attributed to Daniel Webster? And yet, many of our sapient editors keep up the din about this matter, down to the present hour. I have a strong suspicion, that a good part of their credence in this case is *subjective*. They attribute to Mr. Webster, what they might be apt to have

done themselves. It will take a long time, as I hope and apprehend, before the public can be made to believe, that the Defender
of the Constitution pursues a wily, a crooked, a mean, or a contemptible policy, for the sake of elevation to office. However, the
bruit has not yet ceased. It has about as much substance in it as
the Wilmot Proviso, and therefore it is not a matter of any great
wonder that the agitation should be kept up, even after the matter is
explained to the satisfaction of every candid mind.

If any of those concerned in echoing and reëchoing such bruits,
are desirous of knowing how Mr. Webster bears up under such an
oppressive load as this, I can give them some information, inasmuch
as I have seen him, not long since, for a few minutes, and had some
conversation on the point in question. When I witnessed his perfect calmness and dignified composure, it brought to my mind the
story of the *Ox and the Fly;* which, if I may be permitted to tell it,
will convey to all inquirers on this subject, the information they
need, and all that they can reasonably desire. I owe the story to
Burke; but not having his Works by me, I am obliged to forego
the exhibition of his exquisite humor and diction, and to tell the
story as well as I can in my own way. The tenor of it runs
thus:

A stately ox, after satisfying himself, on a summer's day, in a
luxuriant pasture, repaired to the wide-spread shade of a lofty oak,
and there laid himself down, quietly to enjoy his meal a second
time, and to prepare it for digestion. In the meanwhile, a buzzing
noisy fly, which had also taken shelter under the tree, seeing the
soothing quiet of the ox, began to envy him, and finally to make an
effort to annoy him. She lighted on the ox's horn, and there began
a furious buzzing and darting about, hoping to rouse her neighbor
from his repose. It was all in vain. She renewed her efforts, and
made all the racket that such a little creature could make. Still, it
was all in vain. The noble ox kept on, ruminating his pleasant
dinner, and just as quiet as ever. Finally, the fly, determined at
all adventures to attract his notice, spake out and said to him : Mr.
Ox, I beg leave to say, that if I am troublesome to you, and annoy
you, you will be so good as to let me know it, and I will stop buzzing on your horn. O not at all, Miss Fly, said the ox, you have
not troubled me at all ; for I should not so much as have known you

were there, unless you had taken the pains to tell me.   Verbum sat,
etc.

I think we may now leave Mr. Webster under his overshadowing
tree, for the present, where I wish him quiet and undisturbed enjoyment.

By this time, I begin to fancy that I hear some thousands of
voices crying out, and accusing me of being "a Northern man with
Southern principles." Not a word, they say, have you yet said
against the South, but all your arrows are aimed at Northerners.
It seems as if you had drained out the very last drop of Northern
blood that was in your veins. You have turned renegado to your
native soil, and have joined the ranks of the slave-holders, and become their apologist.

But wait, my good friends, until I have finished my task, and then
you will have a better opportunity to judge. I am now going to
say something to my respected fellow citizens of the South; not
indeed in the way of reproach and vituperation and calumny, but in
the way of respectful and friendly and faithful expostulation. I am
one of those who have come thoroughly to believe, that all weapons
in such a warfare, except those of truth and kindness and due
respect, are not only unholy and carnal weapons, but also power-
less and inefficient. I cannot knowingly consent to employ them.

As a counterpart to acts of Northern Legislatures forbidding
their magistrates to aid in the restoration of fugitive slaves, I produce here a law of South Carolina, dated Dec. 21, 1822. The
second section decides as follows :

"If any vessel shall come into any port or harbor of this State, from any
other State or foreign port, having on board any free negroes, or persons of
color, as cooks, stewards, mariners, or in any other employment on board of
said vessel, such free negroes or persons of color shall be liable to be seized
and confined in jail until said vessel shall clear out and depart from this State;
and that when said vessel is ready to sail, the captain of said vessel shall be
bound to carry away the said free negro or free person of color, and to pay the
expenses of his detention; and in case of his neglect or refusal to do so, he
shall be liable to be indicted, and on conviction thereof, shall be fined not less
than $1,000, and imprisoned not less than two months; and such free negroes
or persons of color shall be deemed and taken as absolute slaves, and sold in
conformity to the provisions of the act passed Dec. 20, 1820."

A more recent act of the same State, dated Dec. 18, 1844, declares

that no such person as is described in the preceding act, shall be entitled to the writ of *habeas corpus.*

Let us now place by the side of these acts, a part of the Constitution of the United States.

Art. IV. § 2. The citizens of each State shall be entitled to all the privileges and immunities of citizens in the several States.

Here follows another extract from the same Constitution.

Art. I. § 9, c. 2. The privilege of the writ of *habeas corpus* shall not be suspended, unless when, in cases of rebellion and invasion, the public safety may require it.

Look first at the severity of the penalty, on the captain of a vessel coming into the port of Charleston. One of his colored hands, probably his cook, is taken without any allegation of crime, or even suspicion, and put in prison; and if the captain does not take him away when he sails, and pay all the expenses of his detention, he is liable to a fine of not less than $1,000, and imprisonment for two months. In view of such a process of imprisonment, without judge, or jury, or allegation of any crime, we may naturally inquire, what the Amendment, Art. V., of the Constitution of the United States says :

No person . . . . shall be deprived of *life, liberty,* or *property,* without due process of law.

Due process of law means of course the usual and sanctioned process of examination and commitment for some crime or misdemeanor, by a *regular* court or magistrate. And beyond this ; a law which subjects any one to loss of *liberty* or *property,* must be a valid, constitutional law. If the law of South Carolina, which subjects free colored persons to imprisonment, be not a *constitutional* law, then of course no *due process* can be had under it.

Is it then such a law? No argument is necessary to show that it is not. "The citizens of each State *shall be entitled to all the privileges and immunities of citizens* in the several States." The colored persons who go from Massachusetts to South Carolina, are in all respects *citizens.* They can no more be imprisoned without crime or misdemeanor, than a white man who is a citizen can be put in prison. The statute of South Carolina, then, is *a direct, a palpable,*

an open violation of the Constitution of the United States; it is an affront and an injury of the highest and grossest kind to the State of Massachusetts, thus to imprison one of her citizens, and subject him both to the loss of liberty and of property, without any cause whatever, except the color of his skin.

The crowning part of all, is the suspension of the writ of *habeas corpus*. Such a thing in Great Britain would overturn the government. Such a law is bidding defiance to the Constitution of the United States, and to all the principles of *Jus Gentium*. It has been pronounced, by Judges in the State of South Carolina herself to be unconstitutional. That State was well aware, that she could not stand for an hour before the tribunal of any United States Court. Hence she has refused to let the question of *constitutionality* be carried there. She has expelled one of our most honored and respected citizens, sent by the Massachusetts Legislature to claim our rights and peaceably adjust this matter, without even giving him a hearing. And is this treating the citizens of another State, as *entitled to all the privileges and immunities* of a citizen?

But the case needs no argument. No possible defence can be made for such an infraction of all law, of even all the rights of humanity, and (what is no small matter, and a thing which I should least of all have expected from South Carolina), of the rights of courtesy. Never, never can South Carolina come to us with a good grace, holding an impeachment against us in her hands, for aiding fugitive slaves, while her hands are reeking with the blood of freedom. She must cleanse them, before she can point the finger of menace or reproach at us.

With all due submission to our jurists and legislators, I beg leave to ask, why they have not followed up this matter? Have they any right silently to suffer their innocent fellow citizens to be treated as criminals? If South Carolina be in some respects a sovereign State, and, like the king of Great Britain, incapable as a State of doing a wrong which is cognizable before courts of justice, yet surely it is in the power of the wronged individual, who is a citizen of Massachusetts, to prosecute, before the United States Court there, the sheriff or jailor who deprived him of his liberty and property. If not, then the old maxim of the law, that " for every wrong there is a redress," is not true. In my humble opinion, Massachusetts has no right at all to be silent or inactive in respect to such a matter. The

injustice is so flagrant, that she is bound to aid a wronged citizen to seek redress in Carolina. Surely she must protect her own citizens in the enjoyment of their constitutional rights, or else lose her good name as to impartial justice.

I am no lawyer; but if I read aright the Constitution of the United States, Art. III. § 2, " the judicial power of the United States extends *to causes between citizens of different States.*" What then hinders the imprisoned man from instituting a process for deprivation of liberty and property, before the United States Court in Carolina, against the sheriff or jailor? Their defence would be, that they had acted under the law of their State. But this law has already been decided to be unconstitutional, even by their own Court, and with good reason. Of course, then, the State law is *null* and *void*, and therefore it can protect no one who acts under it. If an appeal is taken from the District to the Supreme Court, by the sheriff or jailor, so much the better. This is the very thing that Massachusetts most of all desires. The question will then receive an *ultimate* decision. If the decision be, as it certainly would be, against the constitutionality of the Carolina law, then has Massachusetts a guaranty of her rights in the United States Executive, who is bound to see that the decision of the Supreme Court is enforced. In this way, it will come about, that South Carolina has not to contend with Massachusetts, but with the whole power of the general Government. The repeal of such an utterly indefensible law, must of course be the necessary sequence.

I repeat it once more in the ears of our General Court, that to my humble capacity it seems plainly to be their duty, to see that the Carolina question be settled by the highest tribunal in the country. Our peaceable citizens are not to be torn from their lawful business, and incarcerated, and subjected to large expenses and loss of time, while we stand by with our arms folded, saying: Will the Lord do good, or will the Lord do evil?

I advocate proceedings in this case, on the very ground of *peace and ultimate concord and unity.* These can never have a place, while causes of bickering and complaint are every day occurring. The causes themselves must be removed. They should be removed *peaceably*, and in an orderly manner, and in a final and conclusive one. What other way so peaceable, so decorous, so promising as to success, as to bring the whole matter before the Supreme Tribunal

of our Republic? If Carolina refuses, why need that hinder us from proceeding in our duty? Let the first colored man of our State, who is illegally seized and imprisoned, without any other crime than the color of his skin, be encouraged and sustained in bringing an action before the District United States Court in Carolina, and let the Commonwealth to which he belongs, see to it that the process is maintained and carried to the Supreme Court. We have then done with the quarrel; and to the President of the United States, our Executive, it belongs, to see that the judgment of the Court is respected. He may be safely entrusted with such a matter.

While I am writing this paragraph, the New York Observer is brought to me, which contains a letter from a "Southern Clergyman," (I presume of Charleston), which undertakes to defend the *constitutionality* of the South Carolina law. As it touches the gist of the question, and contains undoubtedly the sentiments of the leading politicians in that city, with respect to the obnoxious law, I think it proper for a moment to dwell on the main positions which it assumes. He says, (1) That ' South Carolina has an exclusive right to determine *citizenship* for itself.' Very well; I accede. (2) That ' such being the case, she is not bound to deal any better with free colored persons from abroad, than with her own free colored population. These,' he goes on to say, 'when they go out of the State, and attempt to return, are warned off; and if they do not obey, they are taken and subjected to corporeal punishment [i. e. whipping]; and if they still refuse to go, they are to be *sold as slaves.*' So? The fact that there is such a law is true; but how does this prove, that a *citizen* of another State is to be treated in the same manner as the free colored men of South Carolina are? These are *not* citizens in that State, they have no right of *franchise.* Now what does the Constitution of the United States say? It says, that "the *citizens* of each State shall be entitled to all the privileges and immunities of *citizens* in the several States." When this is said, the meaning plainly is not, that a citizen of Massachusetts can go to Carolina, and claim to vote there, or set up himself as a candidate for office. These are merely specialities and appendages of *citizenship*, but not the essence of it. The essence is defined in the Declaration of Independence, viz. " an inalienable right to life, *liberty* and *property.*" This right the Massachusetts citizen, although a colored man, possesses as truly

and fully as any white man. He is a *citizen* in the constitutional sense of that word. Of what use is it then, for the " Southern Clergyman" to tell us, in the way of appeasing our dislike towards the South Carolina law, that she treats our free colored persons as well as she does her own? And how does she treat her own? They are not *citizens*, but a kind of non-descript animals, a *genus monstrosum*. But how can she transmute *our* citizens into this genus? She has no control over *our citizenship*. The Constitution of the United States demands of her, that she shall treat *our citizens*, as she does *her own citizens*, not as she treats her own non-descripts. The right of a colored citizen in Massachusetts to life, *liberty*, and *property*, in South Carolina, or any other State, is just the same as that of her own *citizens*. Nothing but what is local, and which pertains peculiarly to the civil government of South Carolina, with which a stranger of course cannot intermeddle, can be exempted from the demands of the United States Constitution.

It is strange that men of sense, like this " Southern Clergyman," can overlook the evident paralogism which is contained in such reasoning. But, (3) He employs another argument, viz. the right and duty of self-defence and self-preservation. This right, he avers, is inherent and inalienable. Certainly, I reply, if it is reasonably and humanely exercised. But this is an important, yea, an essential condition. The danger must be plainly great and nearly certain, before we have a right to deprive others of liberty, and subject them to fines and imprisonment. But how is Carolina to make out this part of her case? I cannot see. Is the arrival at Charleston of a few colored persons, cooks in vessel-cabins, offensive or inoffensive though they be, a thing to be so dreaded, as to call forth all the thunder of State artillery to stay the threatening evil? But our " Southern Clergyman," says : " We only have the right to judge who are dangerous persons, and to prohibit their coming among us." Be it so ; yet that right, as I have already said, must be *reasonably* exercised, in order to be respected. What if Carolina should say : " We will not suffer an *Abolitionist* to come among us, be he white or black." Is Judge Jay, or the Hon. C. F. Adams, or the Hon. Horace Mann, to be taken up and put in jail, on their arrival at Charleston? Yet according to our " Clergyman," South Carolina can do this, if she pleases. I doubt not she would do it, if she dare. At all events, she might do it with just as much right, in every point of view, as to do what she is now doing.

But there is another point of view, which the "Clergyman" seems not to have considered. What sort of a *confession* is this, which is pleaded as an apology for the law in question? Simply this, viz., that the State of South Carolina is in imminent danger, (for nothing less than this can be a valid apology), of being overturned, or thrown into domestic war, by the arrival of a few dozen of colored persons from the North, who are cooks and sailors. Is this so? Then is this one of the most cogent arguments against slavery, that I have ever yet heard. How in danger? Certainly not from a few cooks and scullions. No, not in the least. But the combustible material is within the edifice of the State, and it needs no more than a cook or a sailor to fire a train, which will blow up the whole building. That is the danger. Our brethren of the South tell us, in conversation and in their journals, that they have not the least fear in the world of the negroes. Why then such precautions as these, which go even to trampling under foot the rights of their neighbors, and violating the Constitution of the United States which South Carolina has sworn to support? They are not afraid, forsooth! So said a gentleman from the South, not long since, to a friend of mine, who asked him, whether he did not sometimes fear that danger was nigh. Not in the least, said he. Afraid? No; for every night, when I go to bed, I take care to have a double-barrelled gun, a cutlass, and a six-barrel revolving Colt's pistol, at the head of my bed. What should I be afraid of? But what, rejoined my friend, if the blacks should set fire to your house in the dead of night, when you are asleep? This question seemed somewhat to embarrass the gentleman; but at length he rallied a little, and replied: They are too great cowards to do any such mischief.

My friend did not press him with any further questions. Had I been there, I could have suggested to the gentleman from the South, some reasons for abating the confidence which he manifested in his last reply — reasons drawn from what I personally witnessed, some 25 or more years ago, in Charleston. I arrived there a few weeks after the plan of an insurrection of the blacks had been concerted, and was within one day of being executed. The plan was, to set the city on fire in all parts simultaneously, in the dead of night; to massacre the whites in detail, as they came out of their houses; and then to take possession of all the shipping in the harbor, and compel or bribe the masters on board of the vessels, to carry them off to St.

Domingo. A servant, who had been treated as a child, out of compassion to his master and his family, betrayed the secret of the conspirators. The leaders were forthwith apprehended, and speedy execution followed. Some 20 or 25 were hung before I left the North. But, for some two weeks before I left home, the papers had ceased to give us any more intelligence respecting the conspirators. When I arrived at Charleston, one of the magistrates of that city took me to his home, with the noble hospitality which characterizes the inhabitants of that city. From a room where we sat conversing, the next day after my arrival, there were visible some hillocks of sand, of considerable height and extent. Pointing to them my friend said: Do you see that highest hillock? Yes, said I. There, said he, were executed our insurgent blacks. Well, I rejoined, and how did the black population behave, who went to witness the execution; and how did the criminals demean themselves? Behave? said he, why they marched by my house by thousands, in perfect triumph. They sung; they danced; they shouted, so as to make the welkin ring. And the criminals? said I. As to them, replied he, they considered themselves as martyrs to the glorious cause of liberty; and so did all the procession. They ascended the scaffold exultingly, and shouting as if their masters were within hearing, they said: Now we are going to have *freedom*, the glorious liberty of the children of God, and you can no more deprive us of that. But how is it, said I, that not a word has been said in your journals, for these three weeks, about the conspirators? For a very cogent reason, replied he, for we found that all the best servants in the city, male and female, were coming forward, and accusing themselves as partners in the conspiracy, even those who were as innocent of it as the child unborn. The spirit of martyrdom had got among them, and they had a burning thirst for the honors of a martyr's death, who perishes in the cause of liberty. The gentleman himself, i. e. my friend, had two slaves, man and wife, who were *inherited* by the mistress of the house, and who had been tempted to go to Liberia by offering to them their freedom and $500 besides, and yet they would not look at the offer. " Massa," said they, " you better care for us, than we for ourselves; we cannot go." I doubt not, from what I saw myself, that there are many such masters and mistresses in the South.

During all my stay in the city, not a black man could appear in the streets, after evening twilight commenced, without a permit in

his hand from his master. The city-guard was trebled and quadrupled. No man could exempt himself from the duty of a watchman; not even the ministers of the gospel or the magistrates. Dr. Palmer, a highly respectable minister of the first Presbyterian church there, told me that the magistracy would not suffer him to hire a substitute. Gov. Hayne himself went the rounds of a watchman's duty, and supervised the whole.

And what does all this mean now? That they were *not afraid?* Why private watchmen of individual houses, in addition to the public ones, were employed every night, in places where danger might lurk. How long this state of things continued, I know not, for my stay there was only brief. But my feelings were much wrought upon by the state of that city. How often did I say to myself: " For all the wealth that sinews bought and sold have ever earned," I would not subject myself to such a condition!

What hold now can any community have, on a population like these blacks, so excitable, so enthusiastic, so capable of being wrought up to a desperate fury, and withal so ignorant, and incapable of feeling any moral restraint? At that very time, there was a law of Carolina, that no black should be taught to read; and of course the influence of the Bible could not be summoned to the aid of peace and good order. But here the Legislature had invaded the high prerogatives of Heaven's Court. Their law was unlawful, antichristian, and utterly inexpedient even on the ground of prudence. A more dangerous policy could not be pursued. It was fore-closing all *moral* restraint upon the blacks. It was commanding masters to do, what Heaven has forbid their doing. " Search the Scriptures " is as much addressed to the colored man, as to the white; and the command is equally binding in every case where obedience is possible. Dr. Palmer told Gov. Hayne, that he should not obey that law. Through *inheritance* his wife owned two slaves, and they had children, who were under his care. He taught them all to read. He told the Governor so; and he, in his gentlemanly and noble-hearted manner replied: Well, Doctor, we are not afraid that you will teach them anything bad. Do as you please, only keep it to yourself.

But to return: what now if the Union be severed, and a civil war ensues, (as it certainly will in case of severance), and the blacks everywhere have arms put into their hands, and are encouraged to revolt? What must become of all those places where the colored

population constitute by far the greater portion of the community? Think of St. Domingo, of Guiana, of Northampton county in Virginia, and other places. But no; I cannot think of these without disturbing my peace. Would God, that all my countrymen were free from all danger, even the most distant, of such scenes as were there enacted!

I have been thus far implicating South Carolina in the charge of having made a law, which is opposed to the Constitution of the United States, and to mutual brotherhood and mutual rights between the different States. I take it that Louisiana has had the same law; but for many years I have heard nothing of it, and therefore must presume that it is repealed. But after all, let us of the North remember, that South Carolina does not stand alone. *Northern* States, in some instances, have as really, although not so flagrantly, stood up in the face of the Constitution. What else is the law of Ohio, and (I believe) of some other States, and the hoped-for law even of our new would-be free Sister, California, but a breach of the Constitution? These States declare, that no free blacks shall come to them, and settle among them. What says the Constitution? It says that the citizens of each State shall have the *same privileges and immunities*, as belong to the citizens of the States to which they may come, while Ohio and other States, say: 'No colored freemen shall ever come among us to settle down.' What difference there is, now, as to *principle*, between this legislation and the Carolina law, I cannot see. It cannot be made out.

Let Northerners then cast out the beam from their own eye, before they cry out at the mote in the eye of South Carolina. Certain it is, that Ohio has immeasurably less apology, (with her views, her light, and her circumstances), for her Acts, than Carolina for hers.

I now take my leave of South Carolina in particular; and in what else I have to say about slavery, I say it in respect to all the slaveholding States in common. But I cannot take my leave of her, without testifying my deep conviction, that there are not, in any State in the Union, among the upper classes of men, in general, persons of more generous feeling, more abounding hospitality, more gentlemanly comity and courtesy, more high-souled chivalry, and more ardent love and pride of country, than are to be found in this State. Add to all this, that she has within her a large number of

true and warm-hearted Christians. I have been acquainted with not a few of her citizens, and can bear personal testimony, as far as my experience goes, and I can truly say of her: " With all thy faults, I love thee still."

There are some other topics which I wish to dispose of, before I come to my *exposé* of what I deem to be the fundamental and irrepealable enactment or principle of the New Testament doctrine, in regard to the matter of slavery. I shall be very brief as to these previous topics.

I do not see but that the South and the North have about equal ground of complaint, as to the journals and periodicals of the day. I do not think there is any room to be worse than many of them are, on both sides. I do not believe that this comes from the fact, that the editors in general are worse than any other class of men. They are everywhere goaded on by partisans, who are aspirants to popular favor. They must yield, or else give up their journal or magazine. Some of them, however, need no spurring on. Every few days we hear of duels among these hot-headed gentry. The only pity is, that nailing to each end of a chest, as is sometimes practised by boxers, is not a part of the law of duelling! Our blessed Republic would, in this way, be rid of some of the most formidable adversaries to its peace, that it has at present in its bosom.

I am certain that nothing can exceed some of our New England journals — some even in the very heart of this Northern domain. I seldom see Southern papers, except in the way of extracts; and there is a plenty of these, which would make any Northerner's blood boil, who has not the mastery over his spirit, and who does not also know, that certain animals which bark loudest and longest, seldom have courage to do much mischief.

But to extend these remarks in respect to either side, over the whole editorial corps, would be great injustice; such surely as I shall never be guilty of. There are certainly not a few of able and gentlemanly and peace-making journals; and I am exceedingly rejoiced to see and know it. As to the *violent* ones, nothing but extremities will satisfy them. All their own points must be carried; and that to the very extreme. If the reign of terror does not soon follow, it will be no thanks to them. They are doing all in their power to hasten it. And all this under the specious pretence of claiming *right* on one side, and *liberty* on the other. Talk of

right and *liberty!* So did the *Sans Culottes* of Paris in 1793. A friend of my early days was in Paris, when Danton, Robespierre, and Marat were in the zenith of their power. He had considerable acquaintance among the Girondist party. When they fell, the guillotine was summoned to new energies. Sixty or seventy in a day were its usual victims. Come, said a French friend to him, one day after its energies had been put to their utmost stretch — come, let us go to the *Place de Guillotine* to-day, and see how our friends the Girondists fare. They went. The first thing which my friend saw, was the gigantic tri-colored banner of the so-called *Republic*. On this was emblazoned, in most conspicuous letters, LIBERTY AND EQUALITY. Soon the heads began to be rolled off from the scaffold. Pray, said my friend to his companion, after witnessing the execution of his Girondist friends as long as he could bear it — pray, what sort of *liberty* do you call this? *Liberty*, Sir, replied he — *Liberty?* Why it is liberty to think as the Directory do, or else to lose our heads. Our liberty is the choice that we have between these two.

Very much like to this, at present, is the liberty of sober, moderate, and peace-loving men throughout our country, whether they live among the fanatics of the North, or among those of the South. It is time, it is high time, that the sober, earnest, patriotic, peace-loving, law-abiding, and truce-keeping part of our community, should rise in the majesty of virtue and united strength, and frown into insignificance the Ledru Rollins and Prudhommes who infest our country, and are preying upon its vitals.

One word as to some men, not unlike these in character, who occupy higher stations, and even find a place in our national Senate and House of Representatives. What painful, what shocking words have we heard from some of them, during the past winter! These are the men to carry with them dirks and revolving pistols, and to produce them (hide thy face, O sun, and look not on it!) in the halls of legislation. Catiline himself would dwindle into a dwarf-agitator, in comparison with them. These are the men to threaten, and to swagger, and to bully, and to brandish dirks, in order to scare the poor Northerners out of their wits, and to suspend by a hair, over the heads of all who are opposed to slavery, the drawn sword of *Union-dissolution*. These are the men to compare our Northern laborers with the slaves of the South, and hold up the latter as

superiors.   And like to them are some of the North also ; men who would hang the apostle Paul for sending back a fugitive slave; men who can seldom utter a word about the subject of slavery without a *tirade* against all slave-holders, or talk of anything but lashes, and starvation, and *Bruins ;* men who scruple not to call every moderate peaceable man of the North, a coward, a renegado, a betrayer of his country, a base deserter to the South, a caterer for good opinion there, and the like.   Such are the *profanum vulgus* of high places, of whom, if one must not say   *Odi*, he may venture to say *Arceo.*   It is such men, on both sides, that for the present moment have got the public ear, and are attempting to ride on the whirlwind they have raised), who, if they are not put down, are soon to steep our soil with blood, and to fill our land with widows and orphans.   It will not do for those who love their country, love peace, love their neighbor although he may have some faults, to fold their arms, and wait in silence the approach of the desolating tornado.   It is their solemn, imperious duty, to rise in the majesty of their strength, and present a united host, which shall scatter to the winds these reckless and boisterous destructives.

Just at the moment of finishing this paragraph, I received another *anonymous* admonition.   My worthy correspondent shows himself to be an ardent Free-Soiler ; and as some one has informed him that I am opposed to insisting on the Wilmot Proviso, and am writing against it, he grows warm in the expression of his feelings, and asks me several (I will not say impertinent, but rather bold) questions.   They run thus : " Who and what are *you ?*   And what have you to do in the discussion of questions that belong to Jurists and Legislators ?   I would, with all due respect, invite you to take the old warning into consideration : *Ne sutor ultra crepidam.*"

I will give a very brief answer.   (1) " *Who* are you ? "   I am a *citizen* of the United States, the most glorious Republic that the sun ever shone upon.   (2) " *What* are you ? "   Ans. Nothing extraordinary, but like most New England men, who love peace and good order and the perpetual union of all the States.   I have in my veins some of the blood which has flowed in the veins of the old Covenanters, in the time of Mary Queen of Scots and James the First of England, and which is still flowing in the veins of some of the Free Church party in Scotland.   Just before I saw the light, the British troops, who burned Danbury in Connecticut, passed by my mother's

door, while she kept at home without attempting to fly. My father was summoned to the army, but the state of his family obliged him to hire a substitute. Near my home, a straggler from the British army for the purpose of pillaging a house, was shot down by the owner, and the gun (yclep'd *King's Arms*) which he had, was bought by my father, and used by me in all my boyish hunting excursions. Often, while I had it in my hands, did I listen to the stories of those who had been in the battles of the Revolution ; and my young blood coursed swiftly through my veins, while I heard narrations about resistance to English oppression. For half a century have I been a citizen of the Union; and what I ardently admired and loved in youth, I have continued to admire and love in riper, in maturer, and in old age. By the favor of heaven, "I am *what I am*" — a republican, a UNIONIST, from the crown of my head to the soles of my feet.

(3) As to the warning, (which, when translated, runs thus: *Cobbler, do not go beyond your last*), I bow in submission to old Horace's authority ; for there was more in him, than what any other half dozen of the Roman poets would make, if they were distilled and their essence combined into one. But then, there is a difference, you know, in the size of lasts; and Horace only says, that no one should go *beyond* his own last. Perhaps I have failed, in respect to finding out the size of mine. Still, in the discussions of Jurists, it sometimes happens, that plain common sense, untrammelled by technics, may make a suggestion that may be useful. Far enough am I, from assuming a place among the jurisconsults, or wishing to invade their province. But I claim a right to utter my humble opinion, when and where I feel a deep interest for my country's welfare. And if jurisconsults, who are warm partisans, happen to read my remarks *adunco naso*, I shall neither wonder nor be offended. Even if they are of the opinion, that I have betrayed my ignorance of political and legal matters, still I beg them to call to mind, that a Phidias, the immortal statuary of Athens, was criticised upon to excellent purpose by a cobbler, who pointed out a defect in the sandals of his magnificent statue-god. If I can do no more than this, even this is doing something.

At any rate, I write neither for fame nor for office. I am aloof from all partisan views, and have no incense to offer with those who cry out: Great is Diana of the Ephesians ! My opinions are not

formed or uttered, with a view to any office which the people can bestow; and I have no inducements to flatter the multitude, nor any special reasons to fear their deafening noise. This is more, than many a member of our national council can say with truth.

And when my unknown correspondent very politely suggests, that I must remember that I am nothing more than a *country parson*, I have the pleasure of telling him that I wish for nothing more. There is not a class of men on earth, to which I would rather belong than to this one; which, however, he evidently means to depreciate. There is not on earth a more honorable employment than theirs; nor is there a class of men more useful, more honorable in the best sense of the word, more pious, or more patriotic than they. Let my lot be with theirs, and heaven knows that I shall deem it " a goodly heritage."

But we must, for the present, dismiss these themes, in order to come to the most solemn and important part of all that I have to discuss, viz., *The attitude in which the radical principles of Christianity now place slavery.*

I shall be very brief; for all that I wish to quote from the records of Christianity may be written on the palm of one's hand. I need, and shall quote, only four texts.

Matt. 22: 39. And the second [great commandment] is: THOU SHALT LOVE THY NEIGHBOR AS THYSELF.

Matt. 7: 12. WHATSOEVER YE WOULD THAT MEN SHOULD DO TO YOU, DO YE EVEN SO TO THEM.

Acts 17: 26. [God] HATH MADE OF ONE BLOOD ALL NATIONS OF MEN, FOR TO DWELL ON ALL THE FACE OF THE EARTH.

Rom. 3: 29. IS HE THE GOD OF THE JEWS ONLY? IS HE NOT ALSO OF THE GENTILES? YES, OF THE GENTILES ALSO.

To these I might add a very significant text in Eph. 2: 14: " For he [Christ] is our peace, *who hath made both one*, and hath broken down the middle wall of partition between us," i. e. between Jews and Gentiles.

These then are the texts, from which I entreat my friends and brethren of the South to let me deliver a short discourse in their hearing.

Christ has declared *all men* to be our *neighbors*. We are to *love them as ourselves*. Love to ourselves is permitted, (not selfishness), and it is taken for granted that we shall exercise it. If we do our

whole duty, we shall as sincerely desire the happiness and prosperity of our neighbor, as we do our own, and refrain from everything that will interfere with it.

Our second text is an excellent commentary on the first, and shows how the proper love of our neighbor will develop itself, when reduced to practice. It is as plain as any commentary can possibly make it, and needs not a word of explanation.

I solemnly invite now my friends and fellow citizens to ponder on these texts. It is impossible for any man to say, that he does as he would be done by, in case he subjects his neighbor, a human being, to slavery. This is not — cannot be — loving our neighbor, or doing as we would be done by. Is there a man in all the South, who is a voluntary holder of slaves, or trafficker in them, who can lay his hand on his heart, and look up to heaven, and, appealing to the God of *love* and *justice* who reigns there, say: I am doing to others as I would be done by, when I compel my fellow beings to labor all their lives for my ease and comfort, without any reward or even a hope of remuneration? Is there one, in that position, who can sincerely say, that he loves his neighbor as himself, when he degrades him from the rank of a human being, and places him in the rank of *goods* and *chattels;* when he cuts off all hope of rising to the possession of any property, or of acquiring any education, or of sustaining even the sacred relations of husband and wife, parent and child, brother and sister? There is not a man in all the South, (that believes there is a God and a Bible of sacred authority), who would dare to say this, in presence of that God *who is no respecter of persons.* This is enough. This test is better than a thousand arguments, and I solemnly and affectionately invite all men, who expect soon to appear before the tribunal of Eternal Justice, to put themselves to this test.

Will it be said, by any, that the African is not a proper man, but an inferior species of animal between a monkey and a man, and therefore we may enslave him, as we do the lower animals? If so, (and this has often been said), then does our third text directly contradict this: GOD HAS MADE OF ONE BLOOD. Besides, Paul has elsewhere declared in the most explicit manner, that by the offence of Adam *all men* were made sinners, (Rom. 5: 19); also that in Adam *all* have died, (1 Cor. 15: 22). There is one God, one Mediator, one Sanctifier of all. Even if the Scriptures had not decided

the point of homogeneous origin, nature speaks it out, in very intelligible language. It is an irreversible law of nature, that different species cannot amalgamate and form a new one, to which the law of continual propagation attaches. But men of all classes and colors can and do commingle and propagate. Beyond this, facts demonstrate the thing in question. The *Jews* in Malabar are black; in China, Tartarian; in Palestine and its neighborhood, of olive hue; in Germany and the north of Europe, they commonly have a white delicate skin, and light hair with blue eyes. Climate changes pyramidal skulls to elliptical ones, woolly hair to long Caucasian hair. The hair on the heads of the negro, is real hair, and not wool, as chemistry demonstrates. These facts are all certain; and being so, they prove that the difference of races is occasioned by climate and adventitious causes, and not by diversity of origin.

I take it that Pritchard, and his Reviewer in the Edinburgh Quarterly, and Balbi, and Adelung, and Mr. Owen of the British Museum, have placed the question about the unity of the human race, as to origin, on a foundation never to be shaken. I have seen, indeed, with deep regret, an opinion of Prof. Agassiz diverse from this, as announced at the late literary meeting in Charleston, S. Carolina. No one more highly respects his talents and skill, than myself. But with the Bible in my hands, and as a believer of its teachings, it is absolutely impossible for me to accede to his views. They are not indeed like those mentioned above, in one very important respect. They do not degrade any portion of men below proper humanity; and this is probably the salvo in the mind of the Professor, which keeps him from feeling that he is arrayed against the Bible. The decisive manner in which he has spoken out against the *transmutation theory* of the author of Vestiges of the Creation, and of the impossibility of one genus passing into another, shows that he is no atheist. May I respectfully solicit, that he would investigate the Sacred Record with as much impartiality and candor and thoroughness as he has the Book of Nature? If he should, I feel certain that he would come to no other conclusion than that stated above, and defended by comparative anatomists of the highest rank. Most assuredly the Bible must be ignored, by any one who concludes that there is a diversity of origin among the human race.

The intellectual and *moral* constitution of mankind establishes a unity of the race beyond all reasonable question. There is no per-

ceptible difference, excepting that which circumstances have brought about, between black, and yellow, and white, and red men. Were not such men as Origen, and Clement of Alexandria, and Cyprian, and Athanasius, and Arius, and Jerome, and Augustine, and others like them, Africans? Not Guinea negroes indeed, but still with hair and skin approaching somewhat near to theirs. And were not the Jews of the yellow-brown hue? Yet intellect springs up in nearly equal measures, wherever it is cultivated and called forth. And as to all the sympathies of father and mother, husband and wife, brother and sister, they are everywhere the same, when equally cultivated. But what is the most decisive of all, is, there is the same *moral sense*, the same perception of good and evil, the same conscience, the same fear of the wrath to come, the same feeling of the necessity of forgiveness, the same hopes of eternal blessedness, the same God and Father, the same Redeemer, and the same Sanctifier. If all these in common do not denote a common origin and unity of the race, I do not know how anything of this nature can be proved. And if all this be true, then, for one part of mankind to enslave another, stands on the simple ground of *might prevailing over right*. Neither the law of love, nor doing as we would be done by, permits any man to act on such a ground, and be guiltless before God.

But we will, for a moment, look at the other *unbiblical*, if not *anti-biblical*, theory. It maintains that the Caucasian race are superior in origin as well as talent. Be it so, for argument's sake. Then where is the liberality, the generosity, the kindness of the stronger, in oppressing and degrading the weaker? It seems as if all these virtues were calling upon the stronger, to treat the weaker and degraded with all possible kindness and tenderness, and to make all practicable effort to elevate them in the scale of civilization and refinement. This is what the gospel demands. It is what Jesus came down from heaven to accomplish; and that same divine Lord and Master requires all his disciples to walk in his steps.

No principle of Christianity can ever be violated with impunity. Heaven has ordained that the way of transgressors should be hard. Accordingly, the evils of slavery develop themselves in a manner not to be mistaken. Let us cast but a single glance upon them, and it may suffice for our present purpose.

(1) It is a glaring contradiction of the first and fundamental principle, not only of the Bible which declares that all are *of one*

blood, but of our Declaration of Independence, which avers, that all men are born with an *inherent and inalienable right to life, liberty, and property*. The South have unanimously subscribed this, as well as the North.

(2) As existing among us, slavery has taken its worst form; it degrades men made in the image of their God and Redeemer, into brute-beasts, or (which makes them still lower) converts them into mere *goods* and *chattels*.

(3) In this form of slavery, all the sacred social relations of life are destroyed. Husband and wife, parent and child, brother and sister, are not known in law, nor protected nor cognized by it. In conformity with this, these relations are every day severed by some slave-dealers, without regard to the feelings of the wretched beings who are torn asunder; and all their parental, conjugal, and filial sympathies are the subject of scorn if not of derision. No invasion of human rights can be worse than this; none more directly opposed to the will of God, inscribed upon the pages of the Scriptures, and on the very nature of mankind.

(4) As the inevitable consequence of this, the mass of slaves must live, and do live, in a virtual state of concubinage; which, so far from being restrained, is often encouraged for the sake of increasing slave-property.

(5) Ignorance profound, and nearly universal, is the inevitable lot of the great mass of all who are held in bondage. In some of the States, the learning even to *read* is forbidden; thus contravening, with a high hand, the command of Heaven to "search the Scriptures." In such a case, obedience to a human law is crime; it is treason against the Majesty of heaven and earth.

(6) The inevitable consequence of all this is, that the young females, ignorant and without a sense of delicacy implanted and cherished, are at the mercy of their masters, young and old. And although the accusation of universal pollution among the masters of the South, is far from being true, yet one cannot walk the streets of any large town or city in a slave-holding State, without seeing such a multitude of mulattos, mestitzos, quadroons, etc., as proves, beyond all possible question, a widely diffused profligacy and licentiousness. It is in vain to deny it. There they are, stamped by heaven with the indelible marks of their polluted origin — a spectacle which might make the sun to blush as he looks down upon them. I know

well that this is a delicate subject. I know well also, that universal and indiscriminate charges of this nature, extended to the whole of the Southern masters, would be utterly false. But I have heard so much testimony in relation to this subject, from ministers of the gospel and Christians who live and belong there, that it is impossible for me to doubt. With my own eyes have I seen the proofs of what I have alleged, in regard to the different classes of mulattos — proofs so ample that no room was left for doubt.

Besides; it is not in the nature of things, that this should be otherwise. Young men in the strength of passion, rendered more intense by a warm climate, having young females at their command, and none to protect or avenge them when seduced, cannot, in any country be kept from licentiousness. They begin it as soon as they are capable; and they continue it, in very many cases, even through life — through a *married* life as well as a single one. Of course the females are undone forever, as to any delicacy or sense of modesty and shame; and Heaven avenges the pollution of the males, by denying them all the exquisite joys of chaste wedded life. Retribution begins here, in this life; but O, what will it be in the life to come? "Whoremongers and adulterers God will judge," Heb. 13: 4. When I think on the utter callousness which such vices generate in the hearts of men and women, the insensibility that is superinduced upon all that is delicate, and refined, and pure, and chaste, and lovely, I might well say with Jeremiah: "Mine eyes run down with tears." If there were no other argument against slavery, this alone would be amply sufficient to secure the reprobation of it, in the eyes of every impartial and enlightened Christian man.

(7) Slavery in its best attitude in our country, even among humane and Christian masters, is a degradation of a whole class of the community, below their proper rank as men. Even where the colored men are free, and educated, and well behaved, they are considered as unworthy of any civil consideration. They cannot become *citizens*, in a slave-holding State. No civil, no patriotic sympathies, can be theirs. "Stand by thyself, for I am holier than thou," is the universal answer to all aspirations after *citizenship*. And this is not all. They are degraded in their own eyes. They are discouraged from all attempts to rise, by a knowledge of the utter impossibility of rising. What were the whole Greek nation, a few years ago, when under the domination of the Turks? Just what

every people will be, who have masters over them, and who are denied their political and civil rights.

Where now did one class of our race obtain a license to keep down and degrade another, when " there is one and the same God of the Jews and the Gentiles ? " And how will they answer before the tribunal above, on which that God sits, *who is no respecter of persons?*

(8) Slavery produces an unhappy influence, on the morals, manners, and temper of the masters. Of course there are many — very many — exceptions to this, where the masters are Christians, and of naturally a gentle spirit. But the habit of absolute and uncontrolled commanding, even from childhood, prepares men to become dictatorial, assuming, unyielding, impetuous, and haughty. It is inevitable. It cleaves to the very nature of such an irresponsible relation. Even good men are sorely tempted and tried by it. Bad ones are made into petty despots.

(9) Another crying evil is, that men grow rich without industry, and become luxurious, and enervated, and prodigal, because they do not know the worth of money, having never labored to acquire it. Hence the extremes of high luxury and degraded poverty, in every slaveholding country. It is impossible that it should be otherwise.

(10) Not only the temporal, but the eternal welfare of the slaves is often grievously neglected. Many masters there are at the South, to my certain knowledge, who are noble exceptions to this remark, and who take great pains to have their slaves instructed in the things of religion. But how many are there, who will never expend a dollar for this purpose? And when these masters appear before Him, who has made one both Jews and Gentiles, and broken down the wall of partition between them, and placed himself in the same relation to all, what answer can they give to Him for neglecting the eternal interests of those for whom he has purchased redemption by his blood?

But enough, and more than enough, on this painful — this revolting subject. When a true hearted Christian runs his eye over such an assemblage of evils, which of necessity stand connected with our present system of slavery, is it possible that he can have a doubt as to what Christianity demands? Can he doubt whether all this is loving our neighbor as ourselves, or doing as we would be done by? No — no — it is not possible. He that runneth may read the will of Heaven, in regard to this matter.

For myself, my childish aspirations, in the very dawn of my life, were all in favor of universal freedom.   I have never changed them; I never can.   In childhood I read with thrilling delight the lines of that heaven-born bard, who, in singing the Sofa, rose speedily to higher themes.   I cannot refrain from quoting some of his thoughts:

" There is no flesh in man's obdurate heart;
*   *   *   *   *   *
He finds his fellow guilty of a skin
Not colored like his own; and having power
T' enforce the wrong, for such a worthy cause
Dooms and devotes him as his lawful prey."

Then after speaking of war and bloodshed for the purposes of ambition and avarice, he thus proceeds:

" Thus man devotes his brother and destroys;
And worse than all, and most to be deplored,
As human nature's broadest, foulest blot,
Chains him and tasks him, and exacts his sweat
With stripes, that Mercy with a bleeding heart
Weeps when she sees inflicted on a beast.
*   *   *   *   *   *
I would not have a slave to till my ground,
To carry me, to fan me while I sleep,
And tremble when I wake, for all the wealth
That sinews bought and sold have ever earned."

Thus feel and think, also, the New Englanders.   How many thousand times have I repeated these lines, and dwelt on the heaven-born spirit which they breathe!   And yet, I have seen and conversed with many a kind-hearted, well-instructed, moral, high-minded Southerner, who wore the appearance of never having once had such sentiments pass through his mind; and to whom such a passage in Cowper would be quite revolting.   What a difference do our early training, habits, and circumstances make in our views!   I could, however, look on these friends with a feeling of sincere friendship and attachment, on account of the virtues which they possessed and exhibited.   I looked on their state as, in very many cases, not a voluntary one, but the result of circumstances over which they had had little or no control.

At present, such is the excitement at the South, roused up by the

violence of Abolitionists at the North, that I can hardly expect a calm and patient listening to my short discourse on Slavery. By and by, when the tempest is past, they may perhaps consent to listen patiently for a few minutes, if nothing more. I do not wonder that they are excited. To be called men-stealers, murderers, tyrants, villains, and every other reproachful name which the rich vocabulary of Abolitionism affords, is enough to awake the dead to life. I view the Abolition proceedings just in the light that I should the following case, which I put for the sake of illustration: I see some fault in my neighbor, who, by the way, has also a great many excellencies of character. But my mind begins to wax warm about his faults, and my conscience greatly presses me to take some measures with him. Well, I hasten to him and say: Neighbor, I wish to have a serious conference with you, on a matter of great importance. When will you hear me? This evening, he says, at 7 o'clock. I go accordingly, and after the usual salutations are past, I say to him: Sir, I have come on a grave errand, that presses my conscience very much. What is it? says he, speak out. Why, say I, it is, that in the first place I expect to prove to you that you are a fool; and in the second place, that you are a rascal. And when I speak this last word, I lay a strong emphasis upon it, and shake my fist in his face. How many ears, now, will this neighbor open, to listen to my rebuke? If he does me common justice, instead of listening to me, he will open his door and say: Sir, please to walk out! When you come to me with proper respect and in a good temper of mind, I will patiently hear you; but never until then.

Is my neighbor now altogether a bad man because he is indignant at such treatment? I trow not. Yet this is the very method in which Abolitionists have assailed the South; and they would be more or less than men, if they were not indignant.

Yet Mr. Webster has been more or less maligned, because he has found fault with such conduct on the part of Northerners. I have not a doubt, that the sentence of his, (in which he expressed his opinion, that Abolitionists had helped to rivet the chains of the slave, and make his bondage the more severe and certain), has roused up more ire in that class of men than all the rest of his Speech. Such men cannot bear to be told the truth, to be told that all this noise and confusion and perpetual vituperation and contumely, are much ado about nothing. With them it is the great,

the only, the all-important business. And all this — is it in conformity with Paul, in my motto? Not quite — not quite, gentlemen.

To me nothing is more palpable than the truth of Mr. Webster's remarks on this topic. I cannot have a doubt, that the liberation of the slaves is put back at least half a century, by this ill-timed, violent, and most injudicious movement. I am aware that I shall of course incur their displeasure. I cannot help it. I think it to be a call of duty, calmly and fearlessly to tell them what I fully believe is the simple truth.

As to Mr. Webster, I imagine he will still continue his repose under his Oak, notwithstanding all the buzzing around him. If he has nothing more serious than this to disturb his repose, I conjecture that he may enjoy quite a tolerable *requiem*. At any rate, I hope this will be the case.

It is time to hasten to a close, although a multitude of questions press upon my mind, in which I feel a deep interest. But it is not for me to discuss everything, and above all the intricate questions that Jurists and Civilians may raise. But I should be doing injustice to my own views of duty, if I did not say a few words on two or three very important topics.

I first address the Northerners, and specially my fellow citizens of Massachusetts. In looking back on the history of slavery in our country, whence do we find it to have originated? From Great Britain; and from her alone. All the Colonies fought pitched battles against it; but the king and Parliament of Great Britain defeated them. North and South were united on this question — united before the Declaration of Independence, and united for a long time after it. I can have room to produce but one specimen of protest; and this is from the pen of Mr. Jefferson, who originally inserted it in our Declaration of Independence which he drew up. It was omitted afterwards merely from delicacy of feeling toward some gentlemen of the South (S. Carolina and Georgia), and also, as Mr. Jefferson intimates *(3 Madison Papers)*, from the same feeling toward some of the delegates from the North, who were engaged in the Guinea trade. Here it is as it came from the hand of Mr. Jefferson. He is speaking of the king of England:

" He has waged cruel war against human nature itself, violating its most sacred rights of life and liberty in the persons of a distant people who never offended

him; capturing and carrying them into slavery in another hemisphere, or to incur a miserable death in their transportation thither. This piratical warfare, the opprobrium of *infidel* Powers, is the warfare of the *Christian* King of Great Britain. Determined to keep open a market where *men* should be bought and sold, he has prostituted his negative for suppressing every legislative attempt to prohibit or restrain this execrable commerce."

The like to this was expressed by most of the Southern States, in one form and another. The general feeling on the subject of slavery at that time, is fully disclosed in the Declaration of Independence at the outset; see p. 57 above. This Declaration has the broad basis of loving our neighbor as ourselves, and of doing as we would be done by — a truly Christian and gospel principle. It is the unquestionable index of all but universal American feeling in 1776.

The Hon. Mr. Chase, in a historical development of slavery in the early part of the United States' career, has exhibited, in his recent, courteous, valuable, and able speech, documents which show that there never was a vote by any Southern State, in favor of slavery, until *after* the famous Territorial Ordinance of 1787. Indeed, I have repeatedly heard it from the lips of some of the Framers and Signers of the Constitution of the United States, that it was then universally understood among all the States who formed it, that slavery was to be got rid of, just as soon as it could be done peaceably and with safety. All the public documents of that period do in fact testify to this. What has made the astounding change? I do not feel myself to be sufficiently cognizant of facts and occurrences at the South, to decide this question; but one thing, I believe may be safely said, viz. that no enlightened Christian people would ever admit or foster slavery, unless they were tempted to it by great prospects of gain. There could be no other efficient inducement.

But there slavery now is, spread over almost one half of the States in number, although not in point of population. THREE MILLIONS OF SLAVES! Who are accountable for this? On whom does the guilt fall? for in the sight of God there must be guilt somewhere, if the declarations or commands of the New Test. are to be our rule of moral appreciation and judgment.

Do not we of the North, often speak on the subject of Southern slavery, just as if the present owners of slaves there, were impli-

cated in the guilt of bringing them there, and placing them in their present condition? Nothing is more common than such declarations. But are they just? Surely they are not. Few indeed in those States have been concerned in foreign importation; and what has been done in that way by smuggling slaves in, has been done more by New England Vessels than by any other. So it was in the Colonial times. Several towns in New England were built up, as every one knows, by the Guinea trade. I doubt not, that there are vessels now employed in carrying slaves to Brazil and to Cuba, whose real owners are New England men. A sham sale and a foreign flag protects them.

In the South only a few have been directly concerned in that iniquitous traffic. What then has the South of the present day done, to increase the number of their Slaves? Nothing, if we speak of the mass, nothing but omitting to free them, and of course they have multiplied by natural increase. If we then of the North are to tax them with sin, as to this matter, we ought, in all fairness, to place the matter on its true basis. Thousands of slave-owners have never trafficked in them; and I apprehend, that the mass of respectable men in the South regard this traffic with abhorrence. Most of the Southern States have prohibited by law the introduction of slaves from other States, although such laws are often evaded. If we tax our Southern brethren with sin, (and I think we have good reason for so doing, provided we speak to them kindly and respectfully), it must be on this specific point, viz. that they have neglected to carry out the design of the framers of our Constitution; neglected to fulfil their implied pledges to the North, in regard to this subject ; and neglected to make any provision for the future abolition of slavery. Nay many of their statesmen have recently declared that slavery is an important, if not a necessary, ingredient in the Constitution and prosperity of a republic. Of course, everything remains in *statu quo*, excepting that the State laws of late have become far more rigorous than before.

May I, with all due kindness and respect, speak a word here in their hearing? Are not the principles of the Gospel, in regard to *loving our neighbor as ourselves,* and *doing as we would be done by,* of high and sacred obligation, universal, irrepealable? I believe every impartial Christian on earth must think and say so. Will it be a satisfactory plea, in the High Court of Equity in heaven,

for disobedience to these requisitions, that this disobedience was profitable to your worldly interests? O never, never! Will it satisfy that Court, when you offer the plea of great inconvenience and much perplexity in accomplishing the desired liberation? I do not think a Christian conscience can be quieted with this. It ought not to be. There is something to be actually done, and done without delay, if you desire to wash off the stain which slavery now attaches to our nation.

What then shall we do? you ask. It is a fair question, and I would God I could answer it, to my own or to your satisfaction. It is immeasurably the most difficult problem ever before this great nation. Universal and immediate emancipation would be little short of insanity. The blacks themselves would be the first and most miserable victims. Stealing, robbery, rapine, and other evils, would inevitably follow in the train of liberation, and thousands of ignorant and starving men would seek their sustenance in preying upon their former masters and upon the community. They could not all be hired, at the prices which they would demand. The ruin of the planters would be inevitable, if high wages for labor must be given. Does not Jamaica tell that tale in deplorable accents? Many an estate has been abandoned. Others, worth £30,000 or £40,000, before the liberation, will now fetch no more than £3,000 or £4,000. Indeed, sales can be made only at prices ruinous to the property-holder. And then, when our slave-holders are thus impoverished, who is to pay the enormous rates necessary to the maintenance of paupers? Plainly, the thing in this shape is an impossible measure.

What then is to be done? Examine, I would say, and weigh well, the plan of *gradual abolition*, recommended by that great orator and statesman, Mr. Canning, when he was prime minister. Had his advice been followed, I doubt not that Jamaica would now be in a flourishing condition. Begin the great work on some such ground as his. *Educate* the young blacks, and let them acquire a moral sense, and become enlightened as to the ways and means of industry.

This would be doing something, yea very much. Make the prospect of eventual emancipation *certain*. Then your consciences will be at peace, and the nations abroad and the North at home, will cease to reproach you.

In the meantime, let the rising *African Republic* be enlarged, until it lines the whole coast of Africa, and thus puts a final end to the increase of slaves by importation. I am astonished beyond measure, when I hear Abolitionists decrying the *Colonization Society.* In what other way is the slave trade to be stopped, and Africa Christianized? All the ships in the British and American navies could not stop the slave trade; and nothing but the *Christian* possession of the maritime coasts of Africa can ever achieve the desired end.

The great wrong of our Southern brethren I think is this, that they have not taken, and do not seem disposed to take, even initiative measures to get rid of slavery, but legislate in order to establish and perpetuate it. But it is too late to accomplish this. The spirit of freedom is waking the world to new life. A new order of things must be near. Shall American Republicans be the last to yield to their fellow men the inalienable rights which their God and Redeemer has bestowed upon them? May Heaven forbid!

I am, I think, pretty fully aware of the great difficulties that lie in the way. Suppose the black population are made free; then what is to be done with them after this, specially in those States, or parts of States, where they are more numerous than the whites; how are they going to live and prosper? They have no money to buy land; and if they could buy it, or have it given to them, most of them are too ignorant, and shiftless, and averse to labor, to manage land with any success. Few of them are artificers; and but few such could find employment. What then I ask the Abolitionists, (and I insist on some plain and direct answer) — what is to be done with such a population? If you say: 'Let their masters pay them for past labor, and furnish them with the means of living;' I ask again: How long would these wages (more or less) last them? As a body, they would never do any more work, until this sum was expended. Then what next? Their masters have been, in the case supposed, already impoverished by dividing among them their property. These cannot, with their habits, carry on plantations at the expense of hired labor. It would reduce them speedily to absolute poverty. And then, what is the next step, either for them or for the free blacks? I insist upon it, now, that the Abolitionists shall give a sober, rational, *practical* answer to these questions. This would be worth ten thousand times more than all their outcries about the sin of

bondage, and their demands of immediate and universal emancipation.

In such a great movement, where the very frame-work of the government and the State is to be taken to pieces and receive a new shape, there must be foresight, and caution, and prudence. One would be apt to think when he hears the clamor for the negroes on all sides, that the rights and interest of the white population are matters of little or no consideration or importance. But this must not so be. At all events, if this movement should be successful, and the blacks be all liberated at once, it would not be long before the fair provinces of the South would be a desolate waste; and the blacks would be by far the greatest sufferers. *Gradual freedom* is the only possible practical measure. Three millions of people cannot be disposed of and provided for, by an Abolition diatribe and decree on paper. In a northern closet, we can sit down, and coolly legislate for the South, on matters that must tear in pieces the very frame-work of their society. We are not affected by any of the proposed measures, and then we coolly wonder why they are so concerned about them. Is this prudence, is it justice, is it kindness, is it loving our neighbor as ourselves?

But I must stop, and leave the plan for remedying the evils in question to wiser heads than mine. It is plain enough, that Colonization, unless sustained by the United States Government at the rate of at least $2,000,000 in a year, can be nothing more than a little canal to empty out the Atlantic Ocean. This work must go on with great power and efficiency, to do anything adequate to our necessities. A noble work has the Society begun; and may heaven grant that the whole country may sustain it and carry it rapidly on. Why not appropriate two millions a year to such a humane, laudable, Christian purpose? It would be but a drop in the bucket. The sale of our new lands would more than furnish the requisite sum. Can any patriotic and humane man object to such an appropriation?

The Abolitionists are continually bringing before us the noble example of Great Britain, as to freeing slaves. It is well. But let us have the whole of it. She gave to the masters *one hundred millions of dollars*, to buy off some 700,000 slaves. At this rate, our slaves would cost the United States $400,000,000. Do the Abolitionists ever say a word about this part of England's example? I have never heard one. No; they flout at the idea of any compen-

sation. What! say they, are we to hire men to do what is just and equitable? But Great Britain said no such thing. She said: 'These owners of slaves came into the possession of property by ways and means sanctioned by the laws of their country. They have, therefore, in the eyes of *civil government*, a just and lawful property. They have committed no misdemeanor, as judged by the laws of the realm, in acquiring it; and we cannot demand that they shall give it up without some compensation, a compensation which is as large as the nation are able to make it.' When Abolitionists begin to insist on this part of British example, then we will begin to listen with an attentive ear.

The last thing I have to say, is, to ask the question, (which I leave to wiser men than I am to answer), whether it would not be a feasible thing, and the best thing we can do, to *colonize the blacks*, as we have the *Indians?* Let them have a Territory and a government of their own, we being merely watchful guardians over their welfare and safety, and for a while reserving the ultimate control of important measures, until they attain to a state in which they will be competent to take care of themselves. Thenceforth we may be their friends and allies, and do them all the good in our power. We have land enough and more than enough to do this; and when done, let us by fair agreement with masters and owners, and proper compensation, stock the Colony until we get rid of the pressure now upon us. It must be a work of time; and it may be such an one. The measure cannot be at once completed. A hearty co-operation of the South would easily effect it; and by its being made gradual, they could gradually accommodate themselves to their circumstances. If any one can suggest a better plan, let him as speedily as may be produce it; and let the measure be under discussion.

I have done with my discussions, and now come to my closing part.

First of all, I ask Christians and all who bow to the authority of God's word, be they in the North or the South, whether any proper regard is paid to the precept: " FOLLOW AFTER THE THINGS THAT MAKE FOR PEACE?" Rom. 14: 19. Let every such man retire to his closet, and open his Bible, after humble and fervent supplication for divine light, and then read, and ponder well, the following texts: " Recompense to no man evil for evil," Rom. 12: 19. " When he [Christ] was reviled, he reviled not again," 1 Pet. 2: 23. " Being

reviled, we bless," 1 Cor. 4: 12. "No reviler shall inherit the kingdom of God," 1 Cor. 6: 10. "THE SERVANT OF THE LORD MUST NOT STRIVE, BUT BE GENTLE TO ALL MEN . . . PATIENT, IN MEEKNESS INSTRUCTING THOSE THAT OPPOSE THEMSELVES," 2 Tim. 2: 24, 25. "SPEAK EVIL OF NO MAN; BE NO BRAWLERS, BUT GENTLE, SHOWING ALL MEEKNESS UNTO ALL MEN," Tit. 3: 2.

Who now can read what issues every day from the press, in journals and pamphlets, or hear what is said in the Halls of our National Council, without a deep feeling of conviction, that no more regard is paid to these solemn injunctions, than would be had they never existed? *The servant of the Lord must not strive, but be gentle.* Is this so? What then is to become of him, who from the pulpit, or the press, and in every possible way, rouses up and urges on to strife, and reviles all men who will not go with him? It is indeed a fearful thing to fall into the hands of Him, "who is our PEACE," and who came to send PEACE on earth, and promote good will among men, after our having violated commands so plain, so practical, so fundamentally important as these.

Let us consider, for a moment, the nature and aspect of the great contest now going on. Here are statesmen, ministers of the gospel, lawyers, respected and honored citizens, men of talents, of integrity, of fair character in all respects, who are opposed to each other from hearty conviction on both sides. The contest waxes warmer and warmer. The Union is threatened and in peril; for even if it is not formally dissolved, it will be virtually dissolved, in a little time, by alienation and bitter hatred. How is such a contest to be stopped? Can either party expect to stop it by insisting on all which he would have, and which he demands? How perfectly idle, and even absurd, is such an expectation! Yet Abolitionists say: 'We must and will have the Wilmot Proviso;' heated partizans of the South say: 'We will have all new States open to slavery; and if not, we will break up the Union.' How are we to remain together, without giving up something on each side? And yet, I do not ask that either party shall give up any thing essential or very important. As to the Wilmot Proviso, we have seen that it of course is annihilated the moment a Territory becomes a State. It is not, therefore, worth one hour of contention. Let us go here with our worthy Chief Magistrate. As to new States

from Texas, (O the dreadful deed of taking Texas and bringing a Mexican war upon us!), there is now no remedy. The solemn compact is made; and therefore it must be kept. There was not a man in our country more strongly opposed to making it, than Mr. Webster; he fought manfully against it; but now his crime is, that he has declared that solemn compacts must be observed.

I ask now all my Northern brethren, whether, in letting Provisos alone, they sanction slavery, or come under any responsibility whatever for it? Not in the least. If the question was, whether they, conceding to them *the power and the right to dictate concerning slavery*, should vote in its favor, then comes a case which is to the point and fundamental. No! No! I say; I would hold out my right hand to have it cut off, sooner than lift it up for such a vote. I would not have upon my conscience the guilt of turning God's image, (redeemed by the blood of his Son, and made free by the Lord Jesus Christ himself), into *goods* and *chattels*. I would not bring on my soul that guilt, for ten thousand worlds. And I am quite certain that Mr. Webster has the same feeling, in its fullest extent.

Nothing else is wanting in the present state of things, but to follow the counsels of Paul, as exhibited above. The North can never lift her hand, to extend the domain of slavery a single inch. But the North must keep solemn compacts, and take care never again to send such men to Congress as will betray her. All the Texas trouble comes from this; for it was two northern Senators that brought defeat on those, who were opposing the Texan Resolutions.

But if heated enthusiasts on both sides, will listen to no caution, and brook no delay of their measures, then let them take the awful responsibility on themselves. I wash my hands of the guilt of my country's blood. And when they have carried their measures, on either side, what is the next step? A war — a war compared with which, the horrors of St. Domingo are but a faint image. — And when the South, by united forces of enemies without and within, is turned to a desolate wilderness, where is the UNION, the once blessed and prosperous and glorious UNION? The North have prevailed; the slaves are free; but how many of them are left, to enjoy their freedom? And where are our white Southern brethren and fellow citizens? Buried beneath the ruins of houses and towns, set on fire and attacked by raging enemies.

This view of dreaded scenes brings to my mind the story of an

eastern Caliph in Bagdad. He had a factious Absalom for a son. He sent him, in order to get rid of his intrigues at Court, into the province of Aderbijan, as governor. He soon heard that he was making efforts, to excite that large and fertile province to revolt. The next news was, that he was in the field, with allied Turcomans as his assistants. The Vizier, who received this intelligence, immediately went and told the Caliph. Call, said he, the commander in chief of my troops. Speedily he came. 'Go,' said the enraged monarch, 'and gather all the forces of the empire that you can muster with speed, and march instantly to Aderbijan, and kill every man, woman, and child there; burn every house, and cut down every fruit tree.' The Vizier dared not interpose for the moment, for his Master's face was black with rage. The commander in chief of the army dared not to interpose. But after a little time, the Vizier returned, and prostrating himself on the earth before the Caliph, he said: Will my Lord suffer me to ask one question? Yes, said the monarch, if it does not interfere with my will and my orders. It shall interfere with neither, said the Vizier. My question is this: When your Majesty has laid your fairest province utterly waste and made it desolate, what domain will your Highness have over Aderbijan? The Caliph dismissed him, slept upon the matter, and the next morning countermanded his orders.

I put now that solemn question to all who are urging the nation on to disruption and a war of desolation: Where will be the domain of the United States, when nearly one half of them is in smoking ruins?

One word more concerning Mr. Webster, and then I have done.

Suppose the violence of the present time succeeds in withdrawing the public confidence from him; and he retires from office and from public life. Suppose even the worst his enemies can wish him should come upon him, and he should go into the shades of retirement, and live and die there, unnoticed (if this be possible) and as it were unknown. The contest goes on, the country is involved in bitter and bloody war, and still his counsel is rejected and despised. But he soon leaves this earthly stage of action and of contest, and is gathered to his fathers, it may be without a monument or a eulogy to preserve his name. If all this can be supposed, and should actually take place; what then? Can the memory of such a man per-

ish? No; posterity, divested of partizan feeling and prejudice, will erect to him a lofty monument, which will be inscribed, on one façade, with these most significant words:

> Justum et tenacem propositi virum,
> Non civium ardor prava jubentium,
> Non vultus instantis tyranni,
> Mente quatit solida.

On another façade, under his simple name, will be carved in high relief:

O NOSTRUM ET DECUS ET COLUMEN!